A Doctor and a Wa

Uncharted Tales of the Iraq War in 2003

'Foreword'

Doctors usually face many battles in their professional and personal lives, with hardly a day passing without a new struggle, whether it be a challenging medical case resistant to treatment or the ceaseless anxiety clinging to the fate of a patient entrusted to their care. Yet, beyond the hospital corridors and on top of these issues comes the daily battles of securing a livelihood and a decent life for their families. In pre-2003 Iraq, doctors were compelled to engage in a different type of war, in addition to the aforementioned struggles, a war they had to endure without having much say in it, like most young people in the country who were crushed by the devastating wars that Iraq experienced as a nation in the past and present centuries.

The most difficult and painful of these wars that one can experience are those with lost cause, which teach the certainty that they will not only lead to military defeat but to a complete and undeniable moral defeat that may erase your country from both the geography and history books, regardless of how you feel towards this country. This type of battles and wars may brand you forever as someone who participated in that historic defeat on the losing side, leaving a profound mark on your memory like a wound that refuses to mend, reopening and rebleeding every time the tendrils of memory brush against the events you yearn to forget.

Not in my wildest dreams I ever imagined that I would have to participate in such a war. The notion of chronicling memories from the abyss of such a war was as foreign as the battles themselves. Yet, the aftermath of this war lingers, a relentless spectre. Not a week unfurls its hours without the haunting spectacles and echoes of that time unravelling in my mind. Over the years, and upon settling in the diaspora, I faced a barrage of questions from friends and colleagues about that period, especially when they learned about my time during this military service. The encouragement from family and these colleagues made me consider documenting those memories, especially as I noticed that some people affiliated with a certain faction or another began to express their views on events of those days without objectivity. Furthermore, I believe that the documentation of these details and events could help in healing those metaphorical wounds caused by this war and the unfortunate events that followed.

Table of Contents

'Before the Storm'

'The Last Night'

'The Torrent of Memories'

'The Military Medical School'

'The Early Days – 1'

'The Early Days – 2'

'Break Times – 1'

'Break Times – 2'

'The Food'

'A Punishment at Dawn'

'The Night Companions'

'The Leisure Times'

'The Amusing Colleague'

'Once Again with (N.K.)'

'The First Return to Mosul'

'An Extraordinary Day'

'Monotonous Days'

'Complete Denial'

'Heightened Alert'

'Lost Time'

'At the Ministry of Defence'

'A Challenging Start'

'The First Confrontation'

'The Boiling Point'

'Ominous Anticipation and Desperate Futile Attempts'

'Major (S) Finally Wakes up'

'The Final Confrontation'

'The Final Escape'

'The Last Day and Night Before the Coalition Military Strike'

'Initial War Days'

'In the Eye of the Storm'

'Finally, We Found It'

'Is This the End?'

'The Final Extortion'

'A Triumphant Return'

‘The Coalition Forces' Offensive Continues’

‘The Siege of Baghdad from the South’

‘Heavy Days Tinged with Fear’

‘The End of the Iraqi Regime is Nigh’

‘The End of the Leave Period’

‘The Toppling of the Idol’

‘The Madness Begins’

‘The Madness and Chaos Extend into the City’

‘Guardians, Thieves or Both?’

‘Return to Medical Duty’

‘Medical Service Adventures - Part 1’

‘Medical Service Adventures - Part 2’

‘Medical Service Adventures - Part 3’

‘Fate of my Close Friend (A.Y.)’

‘The American Protection Unit’

‘The War Ends, but Other Wars Await’

'Before the Storm'

Awaiting storms can prove more arduous than weathering their fury. In the throes of tempests, the genuine mettle and essence of our humanity emerges, and we respond instinctively, laying bare the fabric of our character. Each stride is a testament to the influence of circumstances, often without the luxury of pondering over the dichotomy prescribed by the theories of fight or flight. Yet, on the opposing side, the prelude to the storm bears its own perils, exacting a toll on our physical and mental well-being. We subject ourselves to pressures, mulling over the uncertain terrain of what might unfold or what lies ahead. Picture a tempest not confined to the realms of personal destiny but one that casts its shadows upon the fate of an entire nation. The anticipation, laden with an ominous weight, threads a delicate dance between the weariness of the present and the apprehension of an impending collective future.

I had spent the last nine months of my residency as a rotating doctor at Al-Zahrawi Teaching Hospital, also known as the Republican Hospital, in Mosul, shifting between general surgery, burns, and emergency units from March to December 2002. I recall the summer months coinciding with the FIFA World Cup in Korea and Japan, the crowded hospital lobby during live matches, filled with fans of all the footballing nations taking part in this tournament including doctors, nurses, emergency room staff, and even security officers from the hospital police station, located just steps away from the accidents and emergency department. I struck a deal with my colleague, Dr. A.H., to take turns during our hospital shifts to watch the games of our favourite teams.

As the major teams like France, Argentina, and England were eliminated in the earlier stages of this competition, I, being a life-long German national football team supporter since the age of eight, found satisfaction in witnessing the disappointment of fans of these other teams. This coincided with Germany's unexpected success in the tournament against all the odds, reaching the final against Brazil in Yokohama, Japan. June 30th marked the day when over thirty people gathered in the lobby, with eight or nine supporting Brazil and two for Germany – myself included. The rest were fans of teams that had fallen short in previous stages, perhaps mostly gathered to witness my specific disappointment as I saw Germany lose the final, which indeed happened with Brazil scoring two goals against Germany's none. Of course, I found myself enduring mockery from colleagues.

A four-day delay in the release of our graduation assignment book in October 2000 meant spending an additional three months between October and December 2002 to complete the literal two full years of residency. This seemingly routine procedure had far-reaching effects on the lives of dozens, if not hundreds, of graduates from that academic year, as they would now be subject to mandatory military service starting in January 2003 rather than in October 2002.

The arrival of U.S. military forces in the Gulf region, specifically Kuwait, brought daily news through international media about an American naval fleet entering the Gulf. Despite this, some naively believed that war would not break out. I continued my work and consecutive night shifts during these last three months, hopeful that the military operation would be postponed until I completed my basic military training, making me exempt from the remaining service by paying a sum of one and a half million Iraqi dinars to the ministry of defence cabinet. Everything unfolded quietly, tinged with caution in Mosul, with a gradual slowdown in real estate and car transactions as people began to realize the implications of the presence of U.S. forces. Iraqi television and official media however remained indifferent, deliberately not broadcasting any news in this regard, as if the situation did not concern them in any way.

I tried to convince my parents in every possible way at that time to find a means to escape the country. I even attempted to contact a friend who had family in the Kurdish region in northern Iraq to obtain a passport to escape through that area, but all in vain. During my work in the nearby Baa'aj area, close to the Syrian border, for a month during a previous residency rotation, I reached out to some smugglers in that village. I was on the verge of doing it without telling my family, but fearing that my father, who suffered a heart attack caused by coronary artery sclerosis previously, might have another one if he found out I had to stop this plan while in the very early stages. Those days unfolded in an atmosphere of anticipation and heightened nervousness, a tempest of emotions raging within me. Multiple times, I found myself reproaching my parents for their lack of support for my escape plan. The air was thick with the tension of the impending military service, each moment carrying the weight of uncertainty and the tumultuous blend of fear and longing. As the days slipped through my fingers, the anticipation grew, painting the passage of time with hues of restlessness and a profound yearning for a solution to this pending conflict.

'The Last Night'

Humans, in the face of impending danger that threatens their lives and the lives of their loved ones, often seek refuge in moments of happiness. These moments become a lifeline, a temporary escape from the harsh realities that loom on the horizon. Some, gripped by an insatiable desire, desperately cling to these fleeting joys, immersing themselves in every detail and second, as if under the influence of an addictive recreational substance. It's a frantic attempt to extract the last drop of elation, akin to savouring the final moments and drops of an alcoholic beverage or relishing the concluding traces of a narcotic substance. They strive to obliterate all other emotions and the challenges they face. They plunge into these moments of joy as if seeking refuge, akin to a condemned person embracing their last request or wish before the imminent execution of their sentence. In the throes of adversity, these instances become a brief respite, offering a semblance of normalcy before reality reasserts itself.

The last few days of 2002 were busy with preparations for our family's annual New Year's Eve gathering, which we as a family usually used to spend in a delightful evening with relatives from uncles' and close friends' families at one of our relative's homes. As the year drew to a close, my thoughts were consumed by the fast-approaching basic military training in Baghdad on January 2nd, 2003, a profound tightness gripped me during those waning days, a palpable tension that seemed to intensify with each passing moment. The looming prospect of the coming war cast a shadow over the year's end, leaving me with an unsettling sense of anticipation and foreboding. My late father was the man to go to when it comes to preparing our evening program, arranging the supplies for the games that we, his children and the children of our relatives, prepared for the occasion.

That night at Aunt (W)'s house became a desperate attempt to seize the fleeting moments, as if I were savouring the intoxicating taste of alcohol, even though not a drop passed my lips. I engaged in the revelry with heightened senses, cracking jokes and making comments, my laughter a mask concealing the underlying tension. Every second was savoured, every game and activity embraced, as if an impending sense of finality hung in the air. Everyone asked about the number of drinks I had consumed on that night thinking that the alcohol has affected me. Aunt (W) was as hospitable as usual, and for that night, everyone temporarily forgot about the anticipated war news.

Games continued, accompanied by delicious dishes prepared by Aunt (W) in her Eastern-style home (which I longed for, just as I longed for our home in Mosul), well past midnight. Relatives bid farewell with warm hugs, wishing me good luck in the coming days. Over the following years, I wished to relive a few moments from that night in vain. As humans, we try to recreate such moments in the countries we move to and try to call them home through nostalgia, listening to a specific song, searching for a scrap of paper or a picture from remnants of those memories, or holding onto anything that might carry any kind of such dear memory. We cling to these relics, hoping they possess the magic to transport our imagination back to a time where cherished faces and dear friends or family members, physically distant yet spiritually close, persist in every fleeting second of our days.

The next day, I visit the home of my close friend, Dr. (A.Y.), early in the morning, as agreed, to shave our heads with our own electric razors to avoid shaving at the training centre. We exchange banter, friendly conversations, and expectations for the coming few days. Then, we bid farewell, hoping to meet again shortly in the public transport station to travel to Baghdad. I return home and bid a warm farewell to my family, as if I see them for the last time with a heavily constricted heart. I head to the garage where Dr. (A.Y.) and Dr. (W.W.) are waiting for me. (W.W.) suggested renting seats on a bus, but I eventually persuaded them to pay extra to book the rear part of a taxi to travel quickly between the two cities, especially since the time had reached the afternoon. We all wore hats like those worn by baseball players to conceal our closely shaved heads, but this didn't stop us from ridiculing each other regarding how we looked like.

'The Torrent of Memories'

In the face of challenging circumstances or the impending arrival of difficult times, our memories become the sole refuge we seek. Regardless of their nature – whether they evoke joy or sorrow, warmth or sadness – memories offer a comforting respite amid the icy challenges of our daily existence. Much like the smile of a beloved, capable of dispelling fatigue, or the tender embrace of a mother that washes away the worries of the day, memories provide a sense of warmth essential for navigating the rigors of life.

The taxi glides along the 400-kilometer stretch between Mosul and the capital, Baghdad, enveloping us in deliberately chosen conversations that steer clear of military service. My companions and I delve into a myriad of topics, deliberately avoiding the subject at hand; debating the merits of Zidane versus Figo, determining the supremacy of clubs like Real Madrid, Manchester United, or Bayern Munich, dissecting the latest American blockbuster we've watched, reminiscing about our respective neighbourhoods in Baghdad, sharing insights on the best places to unwind after leaving the camp, and, naturally, indulging in a healthy dose of banter and teasing, particularly aimed at my extravagant choice of taxi. Accusations fly, jests are made, and there's even a suggestion that my profligate spending might lead us to bankruptcy in Baghdad within a few short days if I don't curb my financial excesses.

I attempted to shut my eyes briefly as the car ploughed through the desert, the road carving through it like a knife slicing through butter. Yet, each time I tried, the memories of the past few months and the impending war news flooded my mind, inducing an intense tightness in my chest. I sought solace in recalling some of the joyful moments from recent night shifts and my experiences in the districts of Tal Afar and Baiji, cherishing the amusing coincidences that unfolded with my fellow doctors, (A.A.) and (T.H.), during our work there. I reminisced about spending Ramadan in Tal Afar, where fate handed us dry rations for suhoor, comprising eggs and other essentials, minus any utensils or cooking equipment. In a stroke of improvisation, I concocted a method and a dish for my colleague (A.A.) to have suhoor, given his lack of experience in preparing any type of food. I cooked a dish of meat and fried eggs on the oil heater, utilizing the limited utensils designated for our breakfast which was amusing given that I am Christian and not a Muslim.

I remembered our colleague (T.H.) describing a taxi, a Brazilian VW model, that transported patients to the hospital during the nightly shifts, saying it must be the same taxi every time, and it would be better to disable it so the driver would stop transferring patients to our hospital, giving us some time to sleep. I recalled working at Al-Salam Hospital and the outstanding group of doctors such as (W.A.), (A.S.), (A.A.), whom we called the Blue Leader, (M.K.), (F.Q.), (S.A.), and others. I remembered our evenings and nights together in the doctors' lounge, refusing to return home so we could enjoy playing cards, backgammon, and dominoes. I excelled in playing Konkan (Type of Gin Rummy) and Azneef (A dominoes game), forming a golden duo with my friend (W.A.) that ended the dominance of the duo consisting of the Blue Leader and (M.K.) in these games. I remembered our continued play until the early hours of the morning, after which we headed to some of Mosul's old restaurants to enjoy delightful drinks, kebabs, and more.

Finally, we arrived in Baghdad to move to a taxi that took us all to our respective destinations, which, although different, were relatively close to each other. I arrived at my sister's house and received a warm welcome from her and her husband's family but could tell from their eyes how surprised they were with how I looked after the light head shave for my military service.

'The Military Medical School'

When becoming acquainted with a new place, we strive to comprehend it thoroughly, seeking to assimilate into its essence, and it becomes a part of us. We become a part of its history, and it becomes embedded in our own life. I always remember one of the physics lessons that says when two surfaces of adjacent materials touch, it necessarily leaves an impact on each other's surface. That's how the places we deal with during crucial moments of our life experiences affect us and leave traces that are not easily erased from our memory and lives, perhaps never.

My sister's husband (B.A.) took me to the taxi and buses station from which I would travel to the Basic Military Training Camp, also known as the Military Medical School. The road stretches from the area of this station in an area called New Baghdad through a straight road passing through various residential and agricultural areas without any turns. Al-Rasheed Camp and Al-Rasheed Military Hospital are located on the right side of the road passing through Al-Zaffaraniyah district. We disembarked at the street leading to the Medical School on the left, just before the old Diyala Bridge, a very short distance away. On the opposite side of Diyala Bridge, there are markets, according to what some colleagues described to me.

The school's gate, or what we call the discipline gate, is on the left side of the secondary street that stretches through some eucalyptus trees from the main street where taxis stopped us. The discipline gate was a small wooden room with one or two guards, and next to it was a painted barrier in white and red colours that prevented entry or exit. Upon arrival at the camp, you could see the recruits taking steps toward the gate, while some rushed out to reach the taxis to board them as quickly as possible.

After walking a bit from the entrance gate (also known as the system gate), you reach the ground of the physical training square, and before it, some buildings where the administrative and officers offices are located. On the right side of this square is the restaurant's lobby and store, and on the opposite side are the halls for political guidance offices, in addition to the accommodation barracks for the recruits. On the left side, there are rooms known as the pen rooms, where the privileged recruits who bribe the officers enjoy special treatment, avoiding physical training to stay there throughout the morning, working on written tasks that take no more than an hour.

The school consists of three platoons, and its commander is a Colonel (A) from the Iraqi Army infantry. Each platoon had officers in charge, three of them (Major M, Major A, and Captain A), and the latter was the platoon leader to which I was assigned. Major (M) was lively and light-hearted, while Captain (A) tried to compensate for his lower rank by attempting to appear as a strict officer. There was also a colonel from the Special Forces who visited the school occasionally. This colonel was very strict, issuing many punishments to the recruits and rebuking others publicly in front of everyone. The school had a physical training commander, a first lieutenant from the Special Forces, who assisted the platoon leaders. There were ranks among the infantry permanent recruits, and our chief of corporals (A) was responsible for our platoon. He was known for his staunch and frequent punishments, in addition to his famous saying: "Don't think that you are doctors and pharmacists; you are now here just mere soldiers."

The rotation system at the Military Medical School for us as recruits included two types of alternating weeks. The first type, known as the short week leave), involved attending the school for six continuous days from Saturday to Thursday, with Friday being a day off. The second type, or what we called the long leave week, included two rest days on Thursday and Friday, meaning that the training was only from Saturday to Wednesday. However, we were not allowed to enjoy long weeks until the end of the first month of training.

The recruits who were residents of Baghdad, those from other provinces who stayed with relatives in Baghdad or in hotels there, left the camp at the end of the training day, while the rest of the recruits from other provinces stayed in the school barracks prepared for them. The recruits at the Military Medical School were graduates of medical related colleges (medicine, dentistry, and pharmacy), in addition to graduates of biomedical engineering colleges. On the other hand, all graduates of other colleges and institutes, as well as those without any academic or literary degrees, undergo basic military training in regular training camps. The officers and ranks treated us as recruits far better in the Military Medical School than how they dealt with recruits from graduates of other colleges and institutes and those without any academic or literary degrees in other training camps.

'The Early Days – 1'

I have always relied on my initial perspective and first impressions of a person, thing, or place when dealing with it, and seldom have my initial views and impressions been wrong. Initial thoughts and impressions form part of our instinctive system that helps us survive as humans. We develop and build this system through past experiences and encounters. We continue constructing this system, brick by brick, to create and fortify the first line of defence for our reactions in the face of life's upheavals.

The first day was Thursday 2nd of January 2003. After getting up early around four in the morning, having a simple breakfast following carefully shaving my beard completely, I headed out, wandering among the side streets stretching from the Ghadeer area, where my sister's home was, to the public transport station in the New Baghdad area. The weather was somewhat cold, but not as chilly as it was in Mosul. I was still sensing my slow steps and marking distinctive signs, like some unique houses or shops, so as not to lose my way back on the next day. The area was generally residential, with some shops for basic supplies. There was a large garage for repairing and renting large cargo trucks on the right, extending over a large area. I hear continuous barking of dogs behind the garage fence as I pass by, and I think to myself, what if the gate was open? Perhaps the guard dogs would tear me apart, thinking I'm a thief or someone trying to trespass into the garage.

I arrive at the area where I would take a taxi. The taxi is actually a people carrier van, a Kia or Hyundai brand that accommodates ten passengers in addition to the driver. The fare was very modest by the standards of that time, and the vans were continuously and readily available at this early hour. The cars quickly fill up one after another due to the large number of recruits joining the Military Medical School and the Rashid Camp / Barrack, in addition to those working in the Rashid Military Hospital. The distance is not short, but the straightness of the road and the high speed at which the drivers of these vans (which some referred to as death carts due to the horrific accidents involving any car of this type) drove, along with the lack of traffic on the road at such an early time, make the journey not exceeding fifteen minutes.

Finally, I arrive at the Military Medical School, greet the guards, show them my identification papers and the school enrolment book provided by the Third Recruitment Department in Mosul. They invite me through the gate and point to where I should go to join the rest of my colleagues, awaiting the arrival of the school commander. I see some colleagues and friends from Mosul, stand with them, exchanging soft conversation, and time passes slowly. The process of distributing us into the three platoons according to alphabetical order begins, and unfortunately, I am separated from most of my close friends, as I am placed in Platoon C (the third), while colleagues (A and W) are in the first platoon. What followed the distribution process was a tedious process of checking and recounting the present recruits, sitting cross-legged during the audit and recount process until the first break at ten AM. The post-break period and then noon saw me getting to know some colleagues from Baghdad and other provinces.

In the first week of the training, we were allowed to wear our civilian clothes, so I preferred wearing jeans and a leather jacket during duty. On the following week's Saturday, we returned to the camp, and the process of distributing military clothing to the recruits began. At that moment, I realized how the Iraqi budget was spent on trivial matters. New outfits for all the recruits, and if all those who joined military service over the years were counted in the millions, we would realize the magnitude of the expenditures on absolute nonsense. I didn't like the Iraqi-made military boot that was distributed with the military uniform, so I had to go to the military supply market to replace it with a Jordanian-made boot, paying some price difference. The good thing about this market is the presence of various brands and sources for military shoes and clothing at varying prices, depending on the country of origin. A relative gives me a German-made military jacket from his military service days. Which was one of the top brands and types.

'The Early Days – 2'

As we take our cautious first steps as children, we try to build some confidence in our bodies and the environment around us. Identifying reliable places within a room becomes a crucial task, serving as dependable havens in times of need or fatigue. As we venture into new environments, whether a workplace or a foreign land, colleagues and friends assume the role of these trustworthy anchors upon whom we can depend during our initial steps.

The break times were the most delightful moments in the camp. I gathered with my colleagues from Mosul and those I got to know at the Medical School, exchanging conversations about anything and everything including sports, art, hobbies, video games, and food, except politics and war. However, as the days passed and serious news arrived about the allies in their military operation in Iraq, the conversation took another turn towards military matters, especially since the Medical School was close to one of the military airports. Occasionally, one of our planes would soar through the sky at a not-too-high altitude, allowing us to identify some types by the shape of the wings and fins. Someone would narrate what he knew about this aircraft, when it was purchased, and which military operations it had participated in during the eight-year war with Iran. We talked at length about war-themed video games like Red Alert and Black Gold, which were heavily circulated at that time.

In the company of close friends on the other hand, the atmosphere shifted, as we huddled together in hushed tones discussing the looming spectre of war. Conversations pivoted on the dilemma of whether we hoped for Saddam Hussein's continued rule or yearned for a transformative shift, accompanied by our varied expectations. Amidst this exchange, I found myself standing nearly alone in my apprehensions about change, harbouring an unwillingness despite my acknowledgment and certainty of its inevitability. My concerns stemmed from a deep-seated fear for the nation, wary of the potential descent into chaos under the unfolding circumstances.

In a conversation with us, a Baghdad dentist (A. S.) shared swirling rumours about a potential surge in income and government salaries for doctors if a change unfolded, particularly if the US forces entered Iraq. The speculated amount was a significant leap from the usual $10 per month we received under Saddam's rule, estimated at $700 per month. Friends (A. Y.) and (W. M.) concurred, viewing the change as a preferable alternative to the prevailing circumstances in the country. Expressing my reservations, I remarked that the promised financial gains might come at the cost of numerous lives, and there was uncertainty about enjoying such benefits. Additionally, I raised concerns about the potential escalation of the cost of living beyond the reach of this income increase. I highlighted the looming security vacuum and the risk of extremist ideologies gaining prominence in the absence of effective restraint and control. Contemplating the situation, I questioned whether retaining Saddam in power might be a more stable option, given the absence of explicit state policies or laws against ethnic and religious minorities, even though individual discriminatory practices were on the rise without formal government endorsement. Despite my queries, my friends offered no direct answers, emphasizing their belief in the necessity for change and a fresh start for Iraq, moving away from the stagnation at the time.

'Break Times – 1'

The diversity of colleagues in any work or travel is what gives the experience we undergo with them a distinct flavour, even if we repeat the same experience with different colleagues. For example, while spending time working as a doctor in one of the hospitals, the experience and enjoyment during work vary with different colleagues.

The morning training used to start after roll call, where each group headed by Deputy Officer Hussein or the sergeants or their deputies led us through a series of morning Swedish exercises. After these exercises and a brief run lasting between half an hour and a full hour, each group returns to its usual location to begin the morning training of military marching accompanied by sometimes sadistic penalties for trivial reasons, and usually without any reason.

After the morning training and between other exercises, the officers, ranks, and non-commissioned officers leave us, and we sit on the ground, beginning a Q&A session where non-doctors start asking doctors about various medical conditions. The favourite question was about the sexual act, as if everything we studied for six years in university revolved around this topic. Other questions almost revolved in the same orbit. Have you examined a woman during your medical practice? Have you examined female genitalia? Have you had sexual relations during your service as a doctor with patients or their companions (a subject which was amusing but upsetting at the same time as it questioned our ethical integrity)? Questions full of bewilderment and eagerness for any answer that comes out from any doctor reflecting the state of repression that the vast majority of Iraqi youth experienced, in addition to the great ignorance about such vital matters.

My favourite period was when the questions stopped, and we began humming in very low volume, singing wonderful traditional Iraqi songs like "Elleilah Helwa," "Mihana Mihana," "Kuli Ya Helu," and others. The medical technician (F) and the dentist (S), both from Baghdad, were among the most passionate about these songs. (F) used to tell me that he knew from the beginning that I was an open-minded person who loved music, contrary to the general perception of conservative Mosul residents who tend to be more inclined towards seclusion.

I remember two pharmacists from Amara city in Maysan province. Whenever the sergeant was absent, they would remove the military head cover (beret) from their heads to shake their heads like Iraqi Gypsy dancers with long hair, reciting poetry and imitating the dance of those Gypsy dancers in Iraq. It was very funny, especially since we were all, including the two pharmacists, almost completely bald due to shaving the heads for our military service, and our hair did not exceed half a centimetre in length

'Break Times – 2'

Adapting to and embracing unpleasant experiences often serves as a defensive mechanism for both our nervous and psychological systems. By aligning ourselves with exceptional circumstances, we gradually normalise them, rendering them no longer extraordinary in our perception. Self-mockery and indulging in childlike behaviours are among the defence mechanisms we employ to navigate through challenging situations.

At noon, after finishing lunch, we would get a long break that we fully cherished. The officers, during the morning roll call, would select a few recruits for various tasks, such as working in the calligraphy (pen) unit for those who were skilled in beautiful handwriting, and each group would be given a name, forming what could be called a "circle" or "group."

During this break, my colleagues (A.A, W.M, A.S), and I would form a group to nap a little, or just close our eyes and enjoy the midday sun. To prevent our heads from touching the ground, we would rest them on each other's legs, forming what looked like a circle. One person's head would rest on the legs of another, and so on until the last person's head was on the legs of the first, forming a circle or a loop. Therefore, we called our circle the "Napping Circle," in line with the overall situation,

I usually lowered my beret completely over my eyes, turning it into a makeshift blindfold to block the sunlight from sneaking into my eyes, allowing me to find the perfect position to doze off. This exposed me to ridicule from my colleagues in the Napping Circle, who would say that I looked ridiculous. However, I didn't care at all, as this childish and laughable method was my defence mechanism against the exceptional situation I was going through,

The worst part of physical training was when the officer in charge of the platoon handed over the reins to the sergeant or the deputy sergeant. As they were not degree holders, they would practice the harshest forms of sadistic punishments on the recruits to vent their frustration against those with prestigious degrees like us. They organised running competitions, and those who finished within the last ten recruits would be subjected to various punishments. Here begins the cunning strategy of all the recruits to avoid arriving late and thus falling under the threat of those punishments.

The most favoured punishments that officers liked to apply to us were running competitions on tiptoes and running while in a squatting position. All these types of sadistic punishments led many colleagues to suffer sports injuries, yet abstaining from participating in those exercises or punishments was not allowed. I suffered an injury after two weeks in my Achilles tendon in both feet, which became inflamed due to its repeated and intense use beyond the usual during those training and punishment practices. The officer (A) in charge of my platoon did not accept exempting me from some exercises until he received a jar of Mosul's well known sesame paste (tahini) from my first visit home. When I returned the following week and presented it to him, he exempted me from training for that day. Unfortunately, on that day, our unit was visited by one of the senior officers, known for his strictness, with the rank of a colonel. He ordered us back to training again

'The Food'

On the first day they brought us into the camp's restaurant, they served us for breakfast boxes of milk and cheese with some military bread. I am not a fan of dairy products and don't like most types of cheese, especially the kind that was served to us in the camp. As for the bread, it was nothing short of a hand grenade mistakenly called bread or a roll. The loaf is a greyish block the size of a fist, with some hints of blue and brown colour at the same time. During lunchtime, they served us the same rolls again with a little bit of lentil soup.

On that day, we were forced to enter the restaurant and taste some food. Some of the recruits discovered that some of the dairy products in the morning were already expired. When they tried to confront the officers and commander, the latter argued that it was a mistake in printing. The lentil dish served at lunchtime was supposed to be shared by a number of recruits. Since the camp housed hundreds of them, and the dining room accommodated only fifty people, we were brought in batches, and in front of each group of five or six recruits, a plate of lentil soup would be used times and time again for the next batch. Many recruits especially those in the last batch to go into the restaurant might not even see lentil soup left, but only the remnants of it.

Fortunately, the camp had a small shop that sold some simple foods, such as falafel sandwiches with biscuits, chocolate, and soft drinks. Despite the lack of difference in the quality of the food prepared in the shop and the restaurant, there were some packed biscuits and soft drinks that helped to fill our stomachs, saving us until the end of the day to escape from that hell.

In the first few days, we were forced to enter the restaurant, and the time each recruit spent on a chair there did not exceed ten minutes before leaving, and the next recruit entered with the next batch. I remember the first day well. After the food was served to us, my friends (A.A, W, M) and I exchanged glances without uttering a word. We dared not reach out for any food until we were forced to. Even then, we pretended to eat and didn't complete even a single bite.

One day, (A.A) wanted to try the food in the restaurant, saying that the experience and hardship would not be complete unless we ate something from the camp. I tried hard to stop him, but he insisted, saying, "Come on, my friend, the food here will make men tougher." (A.A) started eating the roll with the lentil soup, and I looked at him with pity. He found some small gravel in the roll, as everyone almost found in their loaves daily, but this did not deter him from continuing. The next morning, when we met, we were all giggled but got worried as (A.A)'s face had changed slightly becoming pale, and him saying, "I should not have eaten in the restaurant. I should have listened to your advice. I had indigestion and stomach acidity all day yesterday, and I couldn't put a bite of food in my mouth all day." That day was the last day any of us put anything from the camp restaurant into our mouths, and we satisfied ourselves with biscuits and soft drinks from the shop.

'A Punishment at Dawn'

My military service began in early January, one of the coldest months in Baghdad. Hence, one of the favourite punishments among officers and sergeants was for us to strip off all our clothes, leaving only our pants. We were then ordered to lie down and assume a position for one of the physical exercises known as "Shnaw" (Bench Press), with arms extended and not allowing us to lie down or rely on our legs or knees to support the body. Factions were assembled in the shape of the English letter "U" in the courtyard in front of the officers' offices to count the attendance of the recruits.

I have fair, pale skin, representing minority of the Iraqi population, perhaps not even reaching half a percent of its population. On one of the days when we were executing this punishment just before dawn, and the sun was rising at the Military Medicine School, darkness still enveloped the courtyard where the recruits gathered. We could barely see through the courtyard to the opposite side where the other platoon recruits were executing the same punishment. My friend (A.A), who, as mentioned earlier, had been assigned to a different platoon than the one I belonged to. While implementing this punishment, (A.A) overheard two fellow recruits discussing something about me between themselves. They said that I would be punished even more because I did not remove the white undershirt from my body in clear defiance and challenge to the officers' orders. The discussion continued for a few minutes, as (A.A) recounts, until he interrupted them, saying that what they assumed to be a white undershirt is nothing but my fair skin. The two colleagues did not believe him at first, but as the sunrise and the first rays of the sun gradually illuminated us while we were still enduring the punishment without any clothes covering half of our upper bodies, they realized the truth in (A.A)'s words. This made them whisper to each other, saying, "Indeed, by God, this is truly his fair skin and not wearing any undershirt." That story became a subject of laughter and ridicule during the lunch break on that day.

'The Night Companions'

The road between my sister's house, where I stayed in Baghdad, and the bus and taxi station where I used to travel from to the camp stretched across side streets connecting the Ghadeer area to the popular market, where the station was located, in a distance of approximately a kilometre. I walked this distance on foot every day, leaving the house around four in the morning or slightly before to make it in time for the morning roll call. The road extended through residential houses, commercial shops, and others for repairing electrical appliances and cars.

One of the shops was a cargo vehicles repair garage that had guard dogs, and I could hear their barks loudly whenever I passed by. However, they never came out, as the shop owner would close the small door designated for them in the main gate at the end of the working day.

On a day shrouded in the pre-dawn darkness, as I ambled slowly towards the station around half-past four, my mind momentarily detached from the present, ensnared in contemplation of my future endeavours. It marked the singular occasion, the inaugural and final instance, where my attention wavered from the path ahead. Engulfed in a sea of thoughts, my reverie was abruptly shattered by the menacing growls echoing from behind, jolting me back to the immediate reality.

A sudden halt gripped me, petrifying me in my tracks. With the utmost restraint, I discerned two onyx-hued guard dogs, salivating ominously, their guttural growls resounding in the stillness. Their intense gaze bore into me, poised to strike at the slightest provocation. Motionless, I refrained from any gesture that might incite their aggression. In the hushed moment, I contemplated the negligence that had granted these ferocious sentinels freedom, perhaps an inadvertently unlatched door. Curses flowed freely, directed at those responsible for this lapse and at the very thieves whose transgressions compelled the shop owner to unleash such virulent guardians upon his domain.

In what seemed like an interminable span, as they stationed themselves merely a few strides away without encroaching further, I initiated a slow shuffle, inching forward with each footfall pressed cautiously into the earth shuffling my feet a couple of inches at a time. Vigilantly, I observed them through sidelong glances, noting their halted advance. Though they refrained from pursuit, the reverberating growls persisted, coupled with their unrelenting and incisive stares trained upon me.

Gradually, I extended my strides, covering a meter or two, daring to take bolder steps, yet with unwavering vigilance. Only after creating a substantial distance, spanning several metres between us, did I resume my natural gait. Still, every step bore the weight of prudence until the gap widened significantly, prompting the dogs to retreat to the confines of the auto repair shop. It dawned upon them that I posed no threat, merely navigating the vicinity and not an intruder encroaching upon their dominion, or more precisely, their realm of labour.

Since that encounter, I've made it a daily ritual to interrupt the flow of my thoughts and maintain a vigilant demeanour whenever I walk past that particular shop. My gaze remains steadfastly fixed on the door, ensuring that my nocturnal companions are not overlooked. This incident evoked memories of a similar episode during one of my night shifts at Saddam Hospital in Mosul, back in February 2001, when I was assigned night duty.

On a rainy night, departing from the doctors' residence and heading toward the emergency unit. In a bid to shield my head from the downpour, I hoisted my white coat and began running and therefore did not make notice of some stary dog lying in the dark on the side of the path while turning right. The dog started barking and running after me as soon as I took the right turn which startled me for a split second. I started sprinting as fast as I could which I jokingly usually describe as this was only possible by activating both the main and auxiliary engines. Looking back to it now, I fancy that I could have possibly outpaced Iraq's hundred-metre sprint champion that night. However, amidst the rhythmic cadence of my own panting, I discerned the approaching footsteps and breaths of an unpleasant companion – the dog.

My main focus was on the emergency department's door, which the guards sometimes used to lock from inside with a key. I began praying to find the door open. As I approached the door, there was a metal barrier separating the street from the door. I jumped over that barrier and pushed the door, and thank God, it was open. With a single movement, I shut door while slipping through which coincided with the dog slamming into it. It was shut completely just when the dog tried to lunge at me in the last moment. I locked the door and, with a sigh of relief, a victorious smile crossed my face. That dog continued to howl and bark for minutes afterward. I thought to myself that night the score was 1 for Sarmad and 0 for the dog.

'The Leisure Times'

My sister's house, where I spent the rest of my days with them after returning from military training, was strategically located. It's one of Baghdad's renowned neighbourhoods, known for hosting numerous affluent families. It was close to emerging and beautiful commercial areas in Baghdad, such as Al-Rubay'i Street, and in proximity to the public transport station that takes me to the Military Medical School.

I was exceptionally fortunate to have my sister's house there, enabling me to leave the camp and reach her place before dusk after the training sessions. Meanwhile, colleagues without relatives in Baghdad had to stay and sleep in the military medical school's dorms, unless they were well-off enough to stay in some nearby hotels.

After getting to know our friend Dr. (A.S.) from Baghdad, we agreed to go out to Al-Rubay'i Street for a stroll. Our meetings there were among the most beautiful times, making that period more bearable for us. We went out to play billiards, sat in cafes, and dined in the bustling restaurants the area was known for. We exchanged light-hearted conversations and banter to momentarily forget the challenges we were going through. Friends and comrades (A.A.) and (W.M.) were the perfect companions for such outings, contributing with their light-heartedness, fantastic conversations, and jokes that filled our gatherings with laughter and entertainment.

Our outings were filled with laughter and amusement to the maximum extent. In that area, we found our haven, a place where our city Mosul lacked such entertainment spots. What puzzles me to this day is how life and people continued with what they were doing without any apparent change or influence from the surrounding circumstances. I mean the lack of a sense, as Iraqi citizens, of any impact from the American and the rest of the coalition forces deployments on our daily lives in Iraq. Life continued as if nothing happened. Entertainment venues continued to be crowded with hundreds, if not thousands, of visitors daily without any change, even in the weeks and days leading up to the war.

While playing billiards / pool and table tennis, we deliberately misbehaved to add mor fun. Specifically, instead of hitting the white ball with the pointed end of the cue, I would strike it from the opposite flattened side, starting a wave of laughter from the rest of the friend. Both (A.A.) and (W.M.) would say, "You've put shame on us among the club regulars. We'll be permanently banned from entering again."

'The Amusing Colleague'

(N.K.) is one of my fellow doctors from the same graduating class of 2000 at Mosul Medical College as myself. He is of Kurdish origin, incredibly kind to the point of naivety at times, and has laziness that goes beyond description occasionally. I remember him during the residency period of our work in the hospitals in Mosul when we shared the same room in the doctors' residence inside the hospital. When we returned from night duty to spend the rest of the night or sleep in the room, as soon as we opened the door or turned on the light, he would start shouting, "Close the door and turn off the light!" repeatedly.

I and the other colleagues always teased him about his second name, (Khosrow), which means king in Persian. It was used to address the Sassanid monarchs like Anushirwan, who was titled Khosrow the First. Since the name (Khosrow) was close in meaning to "loss / lost" in Arabic, I always playfully called him by his name followed by "Khosrow 3-0." I would humorously ask him when he would ever win.

One day in the military camp, after lunchtime, as we were returning to the training ground slowly and waiting for the officer in charge, we saw our colleague (N.K.) in the punishment line with five or six others. The physical training officer, a first lieutenant from the Special Forces known for being very strict, began showering this small group with insults and harsh physical punishment. He ended by saying, "I will teach you a lesson on how to disobey orders so you won't repeat it again." The officer's voice was loud and clear, reaching our platoons where we were standing distinctly.

It was customary in the medical training school to punish some of those who violated orders or committed an offense during morning training. We didn't understand why (N.K.) was being punished with that group. He was not the type to be troublesome or to disobey orders, always correctly dressed in military uniform. Afterward, we heard that they were selected in the morning for not being completely clean-shaven during the morning inspection. We were greatly surprised because (N.K.) was not among those pointed out in the morning by the officers for this reason.

After the verbal abuse from the physical training officer towards this group of enlisted colleagues, the physical punishment phase began. Since the weather was rainy the day before, small pools of water and mud began to form here and there in the training ground area. The punishments, intentionally degrading the recruits with push-up exercises, continued, with the orders that their faces touched the water and mud pools as they descended to ground level.

The punishments continued, escalating to a penalty that involved rolling the body about itself 360 degrees on the ground, like a cylinder, with the process done in water and mud puddles as well. The punishments continued, and we mourned for our colleagues without having the means to stop this shameful humiliation.

The physical punishments stopped, and the officer ordered this group of colleagues to assemble and stand in a single row to resume the verbal abuse. Then he said, passing by their faces and wiping them with his hand, "Why didn't you shave your beards properly? I want one of you to dare to do this again. I will break their back if they do it again." As the officer's hand passed by (N.K.)'s face, he stopped and said to him in an astonished tone, "Hey, who sent you here, and why are you in this group? You are impeccably clean-shaven." Nabeel replied, panting from executing the punishments and perhaps out of fear, "Sir, I was returning from lunch and was a little late. At that moment, I saw this group standing in front of you, so I thought you were going to punish them for being late returning from lunch. Therefore, I joined the line they were in because I saw that happening in the past days to some of the other colleagues." The officer looked at (N.K.) smiling with compassion (it was the first and last time we noticed such a look from this type of officer) and said to him, "My son, go back to your unit. Come on, we're punishing these because their beards were longer than they should have been in the morning, and they were not completely clean-shaven." When (N.K.) returned, and we met him afterward, our condolences and sympathy for him turned into mockery of his extreme naivety when we learned of the full details.

'Once Again with (N.K.)'

Colleague (N.K.) once again is the protagonist of another incident at the Military Medical School. The rules during the first weeks at the medical school were extremely strict regarding leaves. The schedule was six days a week with a single day off on Fridays. As known, basic training is usually a rotation of weeks, alternating between six days and five days. Some recruits, especially those from the provinces of Iraq and the south, began to feel frustrated because the school's commander did not allow them to take their long weekends (when Thursday was a day off in addition to Friday). This made going to their distant provinces impossible over the weekend as instead of leaving the school on Thursday and returning on Saturday morning. However, when the recruits had the Thursday off as well, they could head to their cities after completing training on Wednesday to stay with their families for almost two full days. But the commander officer of the school did not allow this extra day of leave for the full first month.

As a result of this frustration, some recruits began to bribe the officers to go to their cities, while others intentionally skipped and were punished with imprisonment in the camp prison. Our colleague (N.K.) could no longer tolerate the situation. One day he surprised us by announcing that he would travel to Mosul without an official leave or waiting for the school commander's decision to take Thursday as an additional weekend day. He would say, "What will they do to me? No one will notice my absence." We warned him repeatedly that he would undoubtedly be imprisoned, but he didn't listen to us.

The next day, when absences were recorded in the morning by the sergeant, (N.K.) was not present, and he was marked as absent. The same thing happened the following day and the day after that. (N.K.) even took some extra day off and was absent for three full days. At that point, some recruits from Baghdad who didn't know him whispered every time his name was called during the attendance registration, "(N.K.) is not here. Didn't we tell you in the morning that he is not here?! He arranged with the officer from under the table, paid a bribe, and went to his city. Surely, this (N.K.) must be wealthy or have important connections with some senior officers." We, the colleagues from Mosul, secretly laughed because we knew that this was not the truth, and (N.K.)'s naivety prevailed over him despite our repeated warnings that he would be punished upon his return.

At the beginning of the following week, (N.K.) arrived at the school, and when the recruits were being counted, his name was called among the others. As soon as (N.K.) responded with his presence, the commander shouted, "You are punished, and you will spend your absence from school in the school's prison." The rest of the recruits began to look at each other in amazement at (N.K.)'s naivety. Some of them started saying, "Didn't he arrange his matter with them? Why did they imprison him? Is he really this naive to be absent without bribing someone or taking an official leave?"

'The First Return to Mosul'

My enrolment days in military service at the Military Medical School in Baghdad started, as previously mentioned, at the beginning of January, right in the heart of winter and its chill in a city like Mosul. However, in Baghdad, the weather was closer to mild despite a few cold days. What truly intrigued me and opened my eyes to Iraq's climatic diversity was February, which was remarkably moderate in Baghdad, forcing us to turn on ceiling fans. Yet, when I returned to Mosul during this month, piercing coldness dominated the weather there.

Orders were finally issued to allow recruits to take Thursdays off as well, marking the end of the fourth week of training, coinciding with the early days of February. We left the school on that day in a manner closer to comedy, revealing a lot about the character of the officers in charge of the school. We were gathered near the entrance gate, or what is known as the outer gate of the camp, and got counted three or four times. Occasionally, we were ordered to move a few steps towards the gate, only to stop, followed by another command to retreat. These specially designed orders were meant to manipulate the recruits' nerves to smoothly extort bribes in the coming weeks. There were other orders to step back dozens of meters, then a command to advance towards the gate until the final order allowed us to be released from that camp, which had become akin to a prison.

I returned to my sister's house to pick up my bag, which I had prepared the night before, and headed directly to the main transport station where I would ride with friends (A.A.) and (W.M.) in a vehicle that would take us to Mosul. Throughout the weeks when we returned to Mosul, we used more than one means of transportation. Once, we took the bus or what is known as the passenger transport facility, and another time we rode in one of the Kia vehicles. I remember it clearly because these vehicles are known for their high speed, but due to their design, they are prone to frequent accidents. We entertained ourselves during the journey by talking about various matters, while I prayed throughout, certain that my colleagues were also engaged in prayer to arrive safely in Mosul.

I arrived on the Wednesday in the early evening to have dinner with the family for the first time in weeks. I took advantage of the next day to go to Al-Zahrawi Teaching Hospital, where I used to work before joining military service. The purpose of the visit was to collect my monthly salary from the hospital and to visit some friends there. I passed by the emergency unit and then by the second surgery unit where I used to work.

'An Extraordinary Day'

I vividly recall Wednesday the twelfth of February 2003; we had been warned several days prior not to be absent under any circumstances on that day. All those who had bribed their way into non-training assignments, such as office duties, were informed that they wouldn't be able to continue those activities on that day.

Rumours spread that the Military Medical School would be visited by some high-ranking army officials. Others claimed it would be an inspection by the Iraqi Minister of Defence, while some insisted it would be none other than the Iraqi president himself.

A minority knew for certain that this was the visit where members of the Republican Guards would select recruits to join their ranks after completing basic training at the Military Medical School.

The day was heavily overcast with occasional light rain, casting a gloomy atmosphere among the recruits, especially after confirming that the visit would be from the Republican Guards representatives. Recruits were gathered in an amphitheatre-like hall, reminiscent of a theatre or lecture hall.

After cramming the recruits into the left side of the hall, clearing the right side by four individuals donning the red triangle on their military uniforms as a sign of their affiliation with the Republican Guards, one of them began traversing the crowded rows of recruits to cherry-pick those who would later be transferred to the medical field units under the Republican Guards.

The strangest thing happened that day. This man (who held the rank of deputy officer) was selecting recruits only from Sunni provinces, at least approximately 99% of them. Some whispered that he must have had access to our documents before carrying out this task, while others argued that the Republican Guards and some of its personnel possessed keen insight and intelligence that enabled them to easily discern the ethnic origin of recruits.

This deputy officer began passing through the densely packed rows of recruits, gradually approaching the row I was in, the fourth from the end. I buried myself in the chair, hoping he wouldn't notice me. I attempted to cover the side of my face facing him with my hands, trying to appear as if I were dozing off. However, the decisive moment arrived, and he signalled for me to move to the right side of the hall. Thus, I was chosen to join the Republican Guards units.

I collected myself and descended seven or eight steps toward an office at the front of the hall where the rest of the Republican Guards group was noting down names. I informed the group that I would pay the cash equivalent for the remaining military service. However, their response was direct, stating that I could pay it while serving in the Republican Guards units and be exempted from fulfilling the service elsewhere. Colleague (W.M.) was among those selected, while (A.A.) and (A.S.) managed to escape this challenging phase. Fate, however, had something equally challenging in store for colleague (A.A.) later on.

As soon as I returned to my sister's house, I called my family in Iraq, narrating the events in a somewhat comical manner, singing over the phone some of the patriotic songs broadcasted on Iraqi television during the Iraq-Iran War, rallying support for the Republican Guards, especially those that chanted, "Here, O Republican Guard, here, O Republican Guard." Subsequently, we attempted to intervene to have my name removed from the Republican Guards lists through some of my father's friends and cousins, but luck was not on our side, and our efforts failed.

In the following days, I began to feel an intense tightness and frustration, as if death or the angel of death, Azrael, were tightening his grip around my throat. I confided in my family about this, and they tried to reassure me, but the impending war and the misfortune that had accompanied me for some time made me believe that my end was approaching. The problem was that this nauseating feeling clung to me even after emerging from that crisis, and I suffered from its effects for a long period thereafter.

'Monotonous Days'

Life began to return to its monotonous routine at the Military Medical School in the few days following the visit by the Republican Guard members. However, it was evident in those chosen on that day that each one was contemplating, in their own way, how to evade or avoid this selection. Some started using connections and relationships, while others decided to expedite their wedding plans to secure a honeymoon around the same time as their transfer to the Republican Guards.

What changed the negative routine of those days towards something more positive was my attendance of the baptism ceremony of my sister's daughter. I usually spent time with her after returning from the Military Medical School, and many times I had prepared her milk in special bottles. The ceremony was beautiful, and the person in charge of music, or what we called the DJ, played several wonderful songs, including some old tunes from the 1980s.

I also attended the wedding of my sister-in-law's, appearing quite peculiar with a completely shaved head, yet impeccably dressed. I remember my father joining us for this occasion during his visit to Baghdad. On that day, I drove my sister's husband's car and another relative's car between the houses, the church, and the hotel where the reception would take place. My father, who knew the streets of Baghdad well due to his studies there and frequent visits, guided us on the way. We entered one of the streets near the famous Rashid Street in Baghdad due to roadworks and faced difficulty finding an exit. Tensions were visible 0n my father's face, but with a bit of luck and some experience gained from accompanying my sister's husband on his ventures in Baghdad after military training, I managed to find an exit, and there we were on the bridge leading to the opposite side of the Tigris River, where the hotel hosting the reception was located.

Family visits continued during that period, and most conversations revolved around the looming weeks and the impending war—some believed in it while others remained sceptical. However, no special preparations were made by any of the relatives, except for my sister's husband's uncle, who prepared to travel and join his family in Sweden with his son. This was accomplished by the end of February or the beginning of March 2003 when he travelled by land to Jordan.

During one of the family visits, the Palestinian poet and writer Adib Nasser was present as a family friend. Adib Nasser was close to the Iraqi regime at that time, having held various media positions during his stay in Iraq. The visit coincided with a television appearance by the former Iraqi president Saddam Hussein. Adib Nasser secluded himself in a side room to listen attentively and critically to the content of the speech, perhaps to write an analysis or commentary for one of the Iraqi media outlets where he held a position.

'Complete Denial'

Officers and leaders of the Military Medical School arranged a meeting with an officer from the Political Guidance Department, a First Lieutenant. The meeting took place separately with each platoon, and the officer spoke for half an hour or more with each group. He spoke to us about the upcoming war, emphasising the slim chance of its occurrence. Even if a war did happen, he claimed it would be on a limited scale, citing instances when the American air force targeted specific Iraqi sites in the 1990s. He also assured us of the attacking forces' inability to confront our troops openly, insisting that the Iraqi regime, led by President Saddam Hussein, would remain in power no matter what.

He warned us against rumours and their detrimental impact on the morale of our forces. Poor guy, it was evident that he did not believe a word of what he was saying and was only relaying orders received.

Meanwhile, Iraqi television aired interviews with Saddam Hussein meeting tribal leaders from various provinces, especially in the south, showcasing their unwavering support for him. There were also interviews with leaders from all branches of the military, reassuring him about their readiness. However, the most laughable, astonishing, and frightening were the meetings with military manufacturing personnel, where innovative weapons were presented. These weapons were extremely primitive, such as a catapult, locally referred to as "Al-Chatal," and a machine utilising lower limb muscles as a stronger catapult to throw hand grenades over longer distances. These displays seemed like scenes from a surreal and absurd fantasy comedy presented before us. The Iraqi army, once proud of possessing weapons that resisted Iran's vast military arsenal for eight years, was now resorting to using weapons whose invention might date back to ancient times.

I had a sense that the regular Iraqi army was gearing up for a street war, or at least that's what the Iraqi regime was trying to imply. It seemed like the regime was attempting to lure the international coalition forces into prolonging the war as much as possible. The majority of Iraqis did not understand the significance of these displays at the time, and perhaps even today. On the other hand, despite Iraqis' ability to listen to news broadcasts indicating the arrival of new aircraft carriers of the coalition forces in the Gulf and the Red Sea and the deployment of large forces to the coasts of Kuwait, the official Iraqi media and TV channels visibly and audibly ignored what was happening across the southern borders. They continued broadcasting romantic love songs and their usual programs until just two days before the war began, attempting to reassure the people.

The hopes of the regime hinged on a straw, anticipating a decisive stance from the Arab League during a meeting. This meeting witnessed Iraqi-Saudi reconciliation. However, Kuwait, as revealed to everyone, had resolved to participate in toppling the

Iraqi regime. This determination was evident through the events of the meeting, the interruptions between the Iraqi and Kuwaiti sides during their speeches, and the reasons attributed to them. Izzat Al-Douri, the Deputy President of Iraq and the Iraqi representative at the meeting, bore the brunt of the blame from the Kuwaiti side. The final result of the meeting, despite its reassurances to Iraqis and the Iraqi regime's attempt to portray it as standing with Iraq, clearly meant, in the words used in Britain when someone abandons a friend in a difficult situation, "You are on your own, mate." After all the media hype surrounding the conference, no influential decisions were made regarding what Iraq was going through at the time. Perhaps agreements were reached during bilateral and secret meetings on the sidelines of the conference, but in this war, no one would actually stand with Iraq or try to prevent this war. All we heard and saw were slogans and beard-kissing as they say in the Gulf region. We followed the events of this conference at the home of relatives of my sister's husband, who owned a receiver for the Rafidain system, which the Iraqi government allowed to receive through a channel that broadcast the conference. We were able to watch all the details that hinted at what was coming.

The Turkish official position, by preventing the use of their airports, airspace, and Turkish territory by the international coalition forces, increased the Iraqis' confidence in the failure or at least the delay of the war until the convening of the United Nations Security Council, which was expected. It was reported in the Iraqi media that Russia would intervene to prevent any attempt to legitimize the war through them. However, the coalition forces had already decided on war, citing reasons such as supporting terrorism and weapons of mass destruction, charges that were later proven invalid and fabricated one by one.

The Youth (Shabab) Television channel, directly owned and supervised by the eldest son of the former Iraqi president, Uday Saddam Hussein, played a role in reassuring Iraqis about the impossibility or insignificance of the upcoming war. As I mentioned, programs continued to air normally until just two days before the war. It was only then that the tone and programs changed, as if the regime, its members, and its institutions were in a complete state of denial about what was happening around them. They either sought to expose the largest number of innocent citizens by urging them not to leave the country or to divert attention from the impending war professionally. Sometimes, I was personally puzzled over their true intentions, thinking at times that it was an attempt to expose as many innocent citizens as possible by encouraging them not to leave the country, enduring their fates while the storm of the imminent war unfolded so they could be killed in masses which would pressure on the international community to stop the war later on.

'Heightened Alert'

News arrived hinting at which military units we would be transferred to. My colleague (W.M) was assigned to one of the field medical units affiliated with the Republican Guards brigade of the Hamurabi Forces, stationed near Kirkuk, as I recall. As for me, my destination would be the 40th Field Medical Unit, part of the 40th Armoured Republican Guards Brigade of the Adnan Forces, stationed near Mosul. Colleagues (A.A) and (A.S), as mentioned, were destined to stay at the Military Medical School, to be discharged from military service after paying the cash sum to the ministry of defence. Meanwhile, (W.M) and I were to transition to our new military units as soon as the official orders and documents were issued. We would then pay the cash replacement for our service there to be discharged from the rest of our military service thereafter.

Talks about paying the cash allowance and the speed and procedures involved in completing the related transactions became the preoccupation of quite a few recruits. My family was busy arranging the sum of one and a half million Iraqi dinars, roughly a thousand US dollars, in cash to equip and pay it to the headquarters of the Iraqi Ministry of Defence, hoping that the procedures and transactions for the cash allowance for military service would not be suspended due to the approaching war. Everyone was on heightened alert, waiting every day to be called upon so that the procedures for their transfer to their military units could be carried out swiftly. This included terminating their connection to those units quickly if they decided to pay the cash replacement instead of completing the remaining of their military service.

All of this took place at the beginning of March 2003. Our transfer transactions were handed over to the Republican Guard units in the first week for the recruits one by one. I remember the day when my file was handed over, how (W.M) and I, along with a Shiite doctor recruit named (M.H), went to a private office in the Military Medical School to obtain transfer papers to units of the Republican Guard forces. Dr. (M.H) was wearing a stylish and new military uniform with excellent stitching. For some reason, he was very pleased with it and with his transfer to the Republican Guards forces, even though he would still pay the replacement cash in any case. It was as if he were in a state of denial or reassurance that nothing serious would happen in the coming days. I remained puzzled to this day about the reason for his smile and calmness, unlike the other recruits who were dealing seriously and urgently with the situation. They hoped to settle their military service status before the war started, while this colleague did not care whether the orders for the transfer to the Republican Guards units were delayed. After waiting for nearly an hour, I finally got the papers after they were stamped and signed by the camp commander.

'Lost Time'

We finally arrived in Mosul, and the next day I attempted, with urgency, to complete the transaction of paying the cash allowance and be discharged from military service as quickly as possible. This entailed adding a red triangle to the upper end of the arm directly under the shoulders of the military uniform or sewing a new military uniform with this red triangle symbolising affiliation with the Republican Guards. I chose to add the red triangle to my military uniform for time efficiency, and the process took no more than a few minutes from one of the tailors in the centre of Mosul.

Afterward, I took pictures of myself in this uniform, highlighting the red triangle, to be attached to the documents for the cash allowance transaction and military service discharge. Finally, I revisited the Third Recruitment Department, and the place wasn't crowded. However, the First Lieutenant in charge there, upon learning that I was a doctor, asked me to bring him a pain relief medication for a headache while he completed the stamping and signing of the papers.

The Third Recruitment Department and its offices were located near the Municipality of Mosul, a stone's throw from the second bridge, and due to its proximity to my uncle's Pharmacy on Ghazi Street, which represents the natural extension of the old iron Mosul bridge, separated only by the Cornish street overlooking the Tigris River. I walked to my uncle's Pharmacy (D.A) and purchased a box of paracetamol pain relief pills. I then returned to the First Lieutenant to hand him the box, and in return, he handed me the sealed and signed papers, wishing me good luck and thanking me for the tablets.

The next day was Friday, the weekend, and there was no point in visiting government offices as it was the weekend in all Iraqi official offices. So, I took the opportunity to accompany my sister's family, who decided to visit some ancient churches and monasteries, as if bidding them farewell and praying that God would ease the upcoming hardship. The weather was wonderfully spring-like at that time, but I couldn't enjoy these visits as my mind was preoccupied with the damned transaction and being discharged from military service. We visited the Monastery of Mar Mattai (St. Matthew), the Monastery of the Virgin Mary, Keeper of the Seeds, and the Monastery of Rabban Hermiz (St Hermizd), all located in breathtaking areas amidst hills and small mountains overlooking magnificent green plains. Yet, none of these sights managed to take me away from what I was thinking about.

'At the Ministry of Defence'

I returned with my father and my sister's family to Baghdad to complete the transaction of the cash allowance for military service on Saturday. On the morning of the next day, Sunday, March 16, 2003, we headed to the headquarters of the Iraqi Ministry of Defence. The work was bustling in this ministry as if everything was normal. I didn't notice any fear or hesitation on the faces of the employees or the visitors. There were no abnormal or unusual cases, and no movements that raised suspicion or indicated the approaching war.

After waiting in a queue designated for visitors, we were met by a courteous employee with a subtle smile. Upon learning the reason for our presence, she directed us to pay a sum of one and a half million Iraqi dinars to the ministry's accountant. We obtained a receipt for the payment and attached it to the rest of the transaction documents, including my military ID card, known in Iraq as the military service record book, and submitted them in a special compartment.

After a not-so-long wait in the accountant's queue, we finally held in our hands the receipt of the paid amount to the account of the Iraqi Ministry of Defence. We attached it with the other papers as requested by the employee and waited for our turn to see her again. When our turn came, she promptly stamped and signed the papers after verifying the authenticity of the receipt. She wished us good luck in completing the remaining procedures for the transaction.

I couldn't believe what had just happened. All the rumours that the Ministry of Defence would temporarily suspend the cash allowance / replacement system for military service until the crisis was over were ultimately baseless. Is it possible that there might not be a war after all? What is the purpose of assembling all those American and British military units in the Gulf then? Can they gather like this without a purpose? And who will foot the bill for all this after all?

Anyway, there wasn't much left to complete the process of being discharged from military service after detaching from Medical Unit 40. I only needed to authenticate the detachment document from the Ministry of Defence and instruct the Third Recruitment Department in Mosul to stamp my recruitment book as a discharged soldier. All of this could be accomplished in just two days, no more, if everything went smoothly.

That night, the former Iraqi president Saddam Hussein appeared on television, reassuring to some extent those in situations similar to mine. Saddam, in his speech, explicitly stated that there would be no suspension of any transactions related to the discharge from military service or cash allowances. He urged everyone to complete all procedures without delay.

This speech gave me some hope that I could finish all the necessary steps and be done with this nightmare within two days. However, there were no signs of the crisis ending. Everyone in Iraq was waiting for the next few days. I remember there was a meeting of the British Parliament around that time, and they voted in the majority to authorise the British government to engage in the war in Iraq. There was also the final warning from U.S. President George Bush to Saddam Hussein, demanding him to leave Iraq by the night of March 19-20, 2003.

Saddam Hussein's speech, despite personally reassuring me, unfortunately didn't bring any glimmer of hope for a solution to the crisis for the ordinary citizens and Iraqi soldiers. On the contrary, it decisively affirmed the occurrence of the dreaded war, and the coming days would be harsh. At this time, the United States, Britain, and Spain had lost hope in the Security Council and the United Nations reaching a resolution legitimizing the war. Especially after Russia, France, and China announced their intention to vote against any decision aimed at using military force as an explanation or annex to previous resolutions that stipulated the use of the Security Council's means to force Iraq to destroy its long-range missile arsenal.

Despite the strong popular opposition to the military solution through demonstrations and sit-ins in these countries, it seemed that the war was inevitable. After all, there was a meeting held in the Azores Islands between the leaders of the three countries on March 16, 2003. U.S. President George Bush hinted that the hour of truth was approaching, signalling the end of the deadline given to Iraq to destroy all missiles by March 17, 2003. This happened despite the assurances of some officials from the United Nations responsible for the Iraqi file and their inspection teams that Iraq was showing cooperation in this matter. However, Iraq's bet on popular opposition to the war and the lack of cooperation from some neighbouring Arab countries turned out to be a losing one. It threw all its eggs in one basket, aiming to prolong the war as long as possible by dragging the international coalition forces into urban warfare, counting on the convening of the Security Council or the United Nations to stop the war, maintaining the status quo. This turned out to be a losing bet, as we will see later on.

'A Challenging Start'

With the first light of Monday, March 17, 2003, my father and I set out towards the headquarters of Medical Unit 40 for the Republican Guard. Our mission: to finalize what we had started, the completion of the paperwork for my discharge from military service. The plan was to obtain the detachment document from the unit and then head to Baghdad, where the Ministry of Defence was, on the same day. There, the official discharge document would be issued, signalling the end of my military service. Finally, we would return to Mosul on the same day, completing the final stage with a stamp from the Third Recruitment Department.

I had prepared small bundles of money, encompassing various denominations, as gifts / bribes for those working in the records department. The goal was to expedite the printing of my discharge order on the typewriter, enabling me to proceed promptly to the Ministry of Defence in Baghdad in a very short time. The largest bundle was reserved, naturally, for the officer in charge of the unit, Major Doctor (A.A.), and his assistant, Major Doctor (F.A.). Both were from my hometown, Mosul, and while sympathetic to my situation, caution was imperative, decisions needed to be made swiftly, without delay.

Arriving at the entrance of Adnan's forces, I had to proceed alone from there to the unit's headquarters, a roughly twenty-minute walk. Leaving my father to wait with guards at the entrance, I began my journey towards the unit. Fortunately, a First Lieutenant Infantry, who I later learned was responsible for the security of the Medical Directorate of Adnan's forces, arrived in a Russian brand truck loaded with petrol. Upon hearing my story, he offered to take me to the unit's headquarters. I joined him in the cabin, along with the driver, and there was a cramped space, quite uncomfortable, behind the gearbox of the truck. Despite the discomfort, I thanked him, and we continued, albeit with me noticing the truck's sluggish pace.

We finally reached the unit's headquarters, and I bid farewell to the officer and the truck's driver to enter the unit with my bag. The commanding officer was not present at that time, but his assistant took the necessary steps. He instructed the unit's soldiers to swiftly print a discharge order after I handed him the designated financial package. I distributed the money bundles among the clerks who abandoned their tasks to focus on printing the required number of copies of the detachment order.

I hoped for everything to conclude quickly and for the officer to return to affix his signature on the papers. I could then return to my father, who was waiting at the entrance gate. However, during this time, an unusual movement spread throughout the unit. Recruits were scurrying here and there; some tried to organise what they thought needed arranging in the unit. The clerks were attempting to gather scattered papers, creating an atmosphere of professionalism. I wondered about the cause, only to learn that the Officer in Charge of the Military Medical Corps for all units under Adnan's forces, Major (S), was making a surprise visit to Unit 40. They informed me that he was a strict person, and everyone held him in high regard.

It was around nine-thirty or ten in the morning by then. I didn't think this visit would affect my day much, nor did I consider the Officer in Charge and what percentage of a chance there was for an incident that would pit any of us against each other on that day. I sat in the clerk's room, indifferent, contemplating what I had witnessed during the journey from Baghdad to the unit. Families fleeing the capital, Baghdad, with all their belongings loaded on their cars, escaping the impending hell. I felt a deep sorrow for their plight and genuinely wished for their safe return home, hoping for everything to end well for Iraq. At that moment, I reflected on the tragedies committed in the name of freedom, how families were scattered due to senseless wars. I remembered the war that followed Iraq's invasion of Kuwait and how difficult it was for the Shiites in the south and the Kurds in the north. They endured times that could only be described as extremely horrific and tragic, without any gain or benefit.

As I tried to drown in my thoughts, I didn't know the reason behind the accompanying apprehension in my chest. I have always had this hunch and possessed a certain foresight in anticipating events to some extent, but this time, I wished my foresight wasn't accurate. In truth, I didn't know if my apprehension was due to the state of the country as a whole, or if it was for a matter personally related to me, or perhaps both.

'The First Confrontation'

Immersed in my thoughts and apprehension in that room filled with the sounds of typing on the typewriter, I was awakened from my reverie by the voice of one of the recruits at the door. He hesitantly said, "Dr. Sarmad, Major (S) Commander of the Military Medical Corps and Major (F.A.) wish to see you in the commander's office." His voice seemed apologetic, as if he were apologising for something. At that moment, I imagined he was apologising for alerting me to my state of distraction. However, it became clear later the reason for the apologetic tone in his voice.

I left everything and headed to the commander's office, silently thinking, "Perhaps they want to talk to me about allowances and the discharge paperwork." Maybe the Military Medical Corps Commander wants to get to know one of his recruits before they are discharged from military service, especially since he hasn't interacted with me during all the previous events and transactions. The country is about to enter a war in a few days, and he, on an inspection visit, must ensure that everything in the unit, including paperwork and routines, is running smoothly and as usual. Perhaps he will ask me if the unit and its members have performed their roles professionally.

I reached the room, and the recruit asked for permission for me to enter. I was granted permission and entered to perform the military salute, introducing myself as any recruit in the official manner. I said, while hitting the ground with my left foot and my right hand executing the salute, "C.M.S. Sarmad Francis Toma Sir." My eyes shifted between the visitor and the commander's assistant, who signalled me to sit down, and the Major (S) nodded in agreement.

Major (F.A.) spoke again, saying, "Dr. Sarmad, please have a seat. Major (S) would like to talk to you for a moment." Once again, I noticed signs of apology on someone's face, this time on the face of Major (F.A.). It was as if he carefully chose his words, as if he were powerless. As I sat down, I noticed the presence of one of the recruits I had previously met there, the dentist (Z.A.), who had served his entire military service in Unit 40 of Adnan's forces as a conscripted soldier. This colleague seemed disturbed, and his face reflected intense displeasure.

I sat across from Major (S), who began addressing me as follows: "Dr., you are aware of the critical situation our country is going through and the malicious plot that our enemies are trying to involve our country in. But nothing is serious; you know the bravery of our army, and God willing, everything will be resolved in a few days. Even if the coalition forces strike Iraq, it will not go beyond a few insignificant airstrikes to save face. The United Nations and the Security Council have not approved of this war, and shortly, everything will return to normal within a few days or at most a few weeks. Therefore, I have chosen you for a significant national task. You will be the personal physician for Brigadier General and Commander of Adnan's forces, as the man is suffering from high blood pressure, and we need a doctor to be constantly present with him at his headquarters. So, attend to this noble mission."

A smile appeared on my face as I responded to Major (S), "No problem, Sir. Unfortunately, I have already paid the cash allowance / replacement and am awaiting my discharge from military service within a day or two at the latest. Therefore, I will not be of any use to the commander. You should choose one of the other enlisted doctors from the other medical field units of the forces who are still in service."

Major (S) was adamant in his opinion and urged me, saying, "But this is a national mission at a critical time. Do you refuse to perform this national duty? Do you want to falter at this difficult time? Anyway, if you're afraid, don't worry. The commander's headquarters is well-fortified, and any aerial bombardment will not affect it. It is equipped with the best possible comfort, and you will be safe there." I replied trying to reason with him, "It's not a matter of faltering or fear. The issue is that I will be discharged from military service within the next two days, and then you will have to look for another doctor. I'm here to complete the paperwork, and I have already paid the cash allowance. The amount has been received from the Ministry of Defence as confirmed by the receipt in my briefcase, and the clerks are printing my discharge order as we speak. So, I don't refuse, but I'm just saying that I will not be useful in this noble mission of taking care of the forces' commander."

Major (S) responded, "But we need you. Can't you delay the paperwork a bit until things become clear and stabilise? Then we'll issue your discharge order, and perhaps you'll be honoured for your resilience at such a time." I was getting apprehensive at that point and told him, "Unfortunately, I can't. My father is waiting for me at the Oder's gate, and we had planned to go to the Ministry of Defence today to finalise the discharge paperwork from military service." The face of Major (S) frowned slightly, and he said wickedly, "Fine, I've decided to stop and delay your discharge paperwork from Unit 40. We will not sign or stamp it until the crisis is over." I quickly replied, "I'm sorry, Sir, but you cannot do that. Mr President and Commander of the Iraqi Forces Saddam Hussein ordered yesterday in his speech to continue with the cash allowance system for military service as well as not to delay or stop any transactions of this kind. Do you want to oppose his orders? If so, it's your choice, but I will file an immediate complaint to the Ministry of Defence and the Presidency against you and the Military Medical Corps Command of Adnan's forces." I said this with a brave daring smile on my face, confidently relying on the recent presidential speech I had heard myself, and I knew its contents, making me extra confident.

The face of Major (S) stiffened, and his tone changed as he stuttered while responding, "Yes, but the situation has changed today, and we need to have a doctor for the service." I said daringly again, "No, nothing has changed so far; the situation remains the same. President Saddam Hussein's speech was last night, and there has been no new statement or news from the Presidency or the Ministry of Defence regarding this matter. Besides, the forces are filled with doctors, so why me specifically, unless you are trying to go purposefully against Mr. President's orders!?" Major (F.A.) and the recruit (Z.A.) intervened, saying, "Why don't we send recruit (Z.A.)? He is staying with the forces and won't be discharged soon." Major (S) sharply cut them off, saying, "What am I going to do with a dentist? Are you mocking me, or do you want me to become a laughingstock in front of the forces' commander? The remaining doctors are on leave, and I couldn't find anyone other than Dr. Sarmad, and I had to choose him. There's no way around it. Major (F.A.), you have to send him to my unit immediately."

After my initial confident attempt failed and Major (S) persisted, I decided to appeal to him a bit. I said in low humble voice, "Sir, I am the only son of my parents, and both of them have reached an old age. They won't bear the news of my staying here, let alone the news of my injury or death, God forbid, or any harm to our forces." Major (S) responded, "I told you not to worry. The command headquarters is fortified, and nothing will harm you. I guarantee that." I replied almost begging, "But, Sir, if something happens, where do I go with your guarantee if something bad happens? Will you bear the responsibility for my family's tragedy? Will you bear the responsibility for my blood or the blood of someone else? His face changed, and his tone became more insistent as he said, "Nothing will happen; I guarantee that nothing will happen. There won't be a war. The crisis will be resolved within days, and nothing will happen." I responded pleading, "As if you are not listening to the news or the radio. The coalition forces on the borders are preparing for war. They did not come and cross thousands of kilometres just for a stroll. If the situation was going to be resolved and a simple airstrike would save face, they wouldn't have sent ground forces. And in the event of a ground war, the fortified positions won't help us, considering the capability of their shells to penetrate the strongest fortifications. So, all these reassurances mean nothing. This is in addition to the fact that I have already paid the cash allowance, and you cannot deprive me of my legal rights guaranteed by the law and the President's authority."

At that point, Major (S) smiled and said calmly, "Dear Dr. Sarmad, since you do not wish to serve in the military or serve the country in this way, why didn't you try to leave the country, escape, or sneak out of Iraq and go to Europe or America instead of staying?" At that moment, I thought for a second or two that my last solution was to speak in a way that would land me in military prison for a few days. Then, he wouldn't be able to force me to accompany the forces' commander. So, I replied, "Do you think I wouldn't do it, Sir? As long as there are people like you in the country, I will certainly leave as soon as this crisis is over and leave it to you all. I will never return." Such a statement, during Saddam Hussein's rule, especially in the presence of an official like Major (S) and in a government institution like the army and the Republican Guards in particular, was considered a serious transgression, uttered only by someone affected by madness or someone who was a spy for the regime, or close to Saddam Hussein's inner circle, such as officials of the Republican Guards, to test / ensure their loyalty. Major (S) was not certain which category of those he was putting me in, so he answered me, "Dr. Sarmad, you are like my son or younger brother. This talk is very dangerous, and if you had said it in front of any other officer, he would have a different reaction and handling with you. You would have been in big trouble that you couldn't easily get out of. But as an elder brother, I advise you not to repeat it and to return to your senses. Stop repeating such words for your own good. Now, you must obey the orders and come to the forces' commander so that we can present you to him and become his personal doctor afterward."

I responded sharply, "Fine, take me and accompany me to the commander of the forces. I will say the same thing in front of him. I don't care as long as I have a right guaranteed by the law and the authority of the President." Major (S) ended the conversation abruptly at this point and said, "I have decided, and it's over. We will take you to the commander of the forces. Major (F.A.), send him to my office with the medical kit box (a box containing all the necessary medical supplies and medicines in a military medical situation)."

'The Boiling Point'

The Major (S) prepared to leave while I seethed with anger, still saying, "It's okay; let's go to the commander of the forces. Take me to him now, so we can finish this matter immediately and see who is in the right. Come on, take me now." Of course, Major (S) did not respond. He left the unit accompanied by Major (F.A.), who returned after a few minutes to find me holding the papers and orders that the clerks have just finished printing on the typewriter. He stamped and signed them on behalf of Major (A.A.).

I walked to the Order's door after assuring Major (F.A.) that I would return shortly after delivering the stamped documents to my father. I walked in fast steps to the gate where I met my father and explained to him what has just happened. I asked him to go to Baghdad to complete the discharge procedures at the Ministry of Defence while I resolved the issue with the Military Medical Corps Commander and the Adnan Forces Commander. My father left with no delay in a taxi after bidding farewell, and I, unaware at the time whether I would see him again.

It was already noon. I arrived at the Field Medical Unit 40, and Major (F.A.) took me to his room with the dentist (Z.A.). I started questioning them, saying, "How does Major (S) give himself the right to do this? Doesn't he realise it's a clear violation of President Saddam Hussein's orders? Why did he insist on choosing me specifically?" Major (F.A.) tried repeatedly to calm my fears, saying, "It's okay; this is what fate has written for you. Don't worry; maybe this is better for you. We tried with him even before you were called into the office, but it was in vain. When he entered the unit's headquarters, he noticed your presence and started asking about the available doctors to assign one to accompany the Forces commander. We told him there was no one except Dr. (Z.A.), the dentist, who could accompany the Forces commander if he wanted. But Major (S) asked about you, wondering who was waiting outside. We tried to divert his attention and informed him that you would be exempted from military service, waiting for Major (A,A.) to sign your release from the unit. However, he insisted on choosing you for this mission, saying: Stop searching; I found the doctor who will accompany the Forces Commander."

After listening to Major (F.A.) and Dr. (Z.A.)'s account of what happened with Major (S) before I entered the room, my anger and resentment towards him increased even more than before. Major (F.A.) immediately noticed, saying, "It's okay; we will see what we can do. But calm down now; it's not right to go to him in this state." After a moment of silence, Major (F.A.) said, "Tell me, are you hungry? Has lunch been served to you?" I replied, "No, but I have no appetite for any food. I want to end this matter now. Please send me immediately to Major (S)." Major (F.A.) said, "Alright, we'll send you, but eat lunch now. You must be hungry, and you don't know when you will eat again today. Let me order some food for you." I agreed after approving of his suggestion. Major (F.A.) instructed his orders to some other recruits to bring lunch, emphasising that it should be officer's rations.

After a few minutes, a table was set before me with a piece of chicken cooked in red broth and a portion of rice. The food didn't look appetising although it was better than what any regular soldier like me would get from a military unit, but I ate it anyway, fearing that things might escalate with Major (S), and he would throw me into prison. I decided to eat whatever was provided to endure for as long as possible until my father returned with the Ministry of Defence's decision to discharge me. Then Major (S) would be powerless over me, and he wouldn't have the authority to prevent my release.

Although I had finished eating, Major (F.A.) did not go to Major (S)'s office. Every time I asked him about it, he would answer, "Don't rush; we'll send you. Also, the movement's box has not been fully prepared yet. Let us complete its supply with the necessary items, and then we will send you with it to Major (S)." I sat impatiently there in that room, observing the movements of the recruits and officers. I noticed some of the young paramedics and nurses I had worked with in some hospitals in Mosul. I also observed a captain from the infantry, not belonging to the medical corps (not a medical professional), giving instructions to the recruits to dig trenches and arrange some equipment for the unit. Apparently, the unit had moved a few weeks ago to its current location, and it hadn't completed its deployment and settlement in that area yet. The area seemed to have belonged to other units of the Iraqi Army before, as the Adnan Forces had recently arrived after leaving its original base near Mosul. Everything was quiet, and the overall situation was characterised by lethargy. There was nothing being accomplished quickly, and signs of the upcoming war were only evident on the faces of some recruits who were filled with confusion and apprehension about the unknown future.

At two o'clock, one of the recruits came complaining about a medical condition. Major (F.A.) turned to me, saying in apologetic tone, "You know well, Dr. Sarmad, that our military medical knowledge has almost expired, and we are no longer updated on the latest information and developments. Only the title remains from the profession. Can you please examine him if possible?" I complied and prescribed the appropriate medication after a brief examination. At three o'clock, as my patience was running out, Major (F.A.) informed me that the time had arrived, and now they could send me to Major (S).

'Ominous Anticipation and Desperate Futile Attempts'

Some of the soldiers in the medical field unit 40 loaded the movement box into the rear bed of a small Toyota pickup vehicle, the Deluxe model. I took the seat next to the driver while three soldiers boarded the rear bed alongside the movement box. After a somewhat slow drive for about ten minutes, we arrived at a single-story building surrounded by a beautifully landscaped garden. There was a military-coloured Toyota Land Cruiser with an ambulance and a few small cargo and pickup vehicles scattered around it. Some soldiers were scattered here and there, some washing a vehicle, and others engrossed in different tasks. The seriousness on the soldiers' faces was palpable, with no slack in their work, everyone appearing or at lest trying to appear deeply engrossed in some task.

I inquired about the whereabouts of Major (S), and they pointed to the building, saying he was in the command headquarters of Adnan's military medical corps in that building. I headed towards the building and when I reached there I noticed the first lieutenant who helped me earlier in the day walking very slowly in the garden. I reached up to some soldiers standing at the inner gate of the building's garden and requested permission to be allowed in. One of them, Deputy Officer (A), answered me, asking what I wanted. I quickly recounted what had happened to me and how Major (S) ordered me to accompany the forces' commander against my will, violating the explicit instructions and directives of the Iraqi president the day before. I was speaking in a loud voice on purpose to alert the first lieutenant to my plight. The surprise was evident on the deputy officer (A)'s face; he did not respond with words but remained silent, perhaps thinking, "Who is this madman daring to narrate such an incident in front of the security officer and an officer like Major (S)?" He only murmured "Major (S) is sleeping". I asked the deputy officer to wake Major (S) up when he looked in disbelief and even horror at me as if he was saying who would dare to do such as stupid thing. He only mumbled: "Major (S) has strict orders not to wake him up from his afternoon naps, no one can do this in their right mind".

I continued my complaint, saying, "Sir, would you approve of what's happening to me? Is it right to ignore our president's instructions and force me into such a matter? On top of all this, Major (S) wants to halt the processing of my military service discharge despite the authenticity of all the documents and procedures I've completed? I then pleaded with the first lieutenant (who was in fact the security officer of the forces as well) who by then has made his way to where I had the conversation with deputy officer saying: "Sir, I'll make you a witness. Please accompany us to the forces' commander to give your opinion. Is it right for us to defy the instructions of the President of the Republic? This is a blatant violation of those orders. I'll mention all this in front of the forces' commander, and I'm sure he'll vindicate me. After all the nerve-wracking situation I was in, I was just told by the deputy officer (A) that Major (S) is sleeping, leaving me in such a dire situation without any sense of responsibility. I'll also complain about this. It's a disregard for the rights and lives of others."

What I said sounded like verbal diarrhoea from someone who had lost control of their nerves, teetering on the edge of a severe nervous breakdown. But at the same time, it was a measured speech that no one, including the forces' commander, could easily dismiss, potentially and hence could not lead to a delay to my military service discharge in the midst of all these critical times.

These words left the first lieutenant perplexed about me, apparently. His eyes widened as he looked at me in amazement, perhaps wondering whether I was insane or an infiltrator trying to spy for the regime or the ministry of defence on its officers in such a sensitive situation. He spoke only a few words, saying, "Wait for Major (S) and try to resolve the issue with him." It was clear that he was trying to avoid a potential confrontation with Major (S) or intervening in a matter that might involve issues beyond his capacity if it turned out that I was a spy for the ministry. He shifted his gaze away, trying to calm me and advise me to wait for Major (S).

'Major (S) Finally Wakes up'

Three agonizing and tedious hours had passed in which I couldn't find a moment of calm. I could feel the adrenaline coursing through me, occupying perhaps half the volume of my circulatory system. I paced in front of the building of Adnan's military medical command, coming and going hundreds if not possibly thousands of times. At times, I immersed myself in my dark thoughts, especially since I felt or envisioned how the angel of death was pursuing me, drawing closer with each passing month and week. My mental state began to deteriorate amid these thoughts and feelings. I felt that I wouldn't emerge alive or unscathed from this ordeal. Perhaps, this was the first real test of my nerve strength. Yes, I emerged from it intact and victorious later on, but its negative effects lingered until this day. To describe it scientifically, I can say that maybe the psychological shock my body experienced that day, coupled with the conflicting emotions of optimism and pessimism, smiles and scowls, joy and deep sorrow, melancholic feelings and a sense of injustice, and the loss of hope – all clashed within me in a brief period not exceeding a few hours that day. That experience was more significant and stronger than what my unaccustomed body could bear, facing such a quantity of conflicting events in a single day. I almost assert that the impact of that day is still present in my body and my subconscious mind. Perhaps the true impact will only become clear after years and years. I almost assert that if I ever suffer from a state of chronic depression in the future, its beginnings might be traced back to that strange day.

My eyes closely monitored the building's door, casting a glance at it now and then, and whenever any sound emanated from that building, I would leap, directing my gaze towards it, hoping to see Major (S) and end this deadly nightmare. Around half-past six, the door finally moved, and Major (S) emerged, holding his military cap in his hand, attempting to secure it on his head. As he approached, I rendered him the military salute, and with a smile, he said, "Hello choc, hello Doc, what brings you here at half-past six?" The meaning of his words was, "Hello chocolate, hello doctor, what should I do with you now that you've come to me at half-past six?" I replied, "Sir, I requested them at the medical field unit 40 to send me to you earlier to resolve the matter, but they didn't do so until three in the afternoon, and no one dared to disturb your sleep. So, you see me now in front of you. But it's okay, take me to the forces' commander, as I want to conclude this matter immediately, so I can return to my family not too late, as I still have a journey ahead, either to Baghdad or Mosul." Major (S) responded with a wicked smile, "What should I do with you at this time? No, I won't take you with me. I have a meeting with the forces' commander, and I'll look into your matter when I return." I said to him, "But since you're going there, isn't it possibly more efficient to take me with you at once? I don't want the time to be delayed any further, if possible, as I have a journey ahead." He answered, "No, our meeting is for another purpose. You must wait here until I return." I asked, "And how long will that meeting take?" He replied, "An hour or so. You'll stay, and this is my final decision."

I watched in despair Major (S) as he distanced himself in a four-wheel drive vehicle, and the dark thoughts resumed their dance and sway in my mind. I wondered, "What will he decide about me when he returns? Perhaps, he will punish me with lashes for daring to complain about him to the forces' commander. Undoubtedly, my words reached him, and he desires to personally torture me upon his return. Possibly there would be a punishment of a completely different type. Who knows how this creepy creature thinks?"

'The Final Confrontation'

My patience began to wear thin as time passed, and my nerves intensified as I paced through the garden and the adjacent courtyard, my head lowered, contemplating all possibilities. Could I deceive the guards and soldiers to escape if I wanted to? Or would it only worsen my problems if I did? When will Major (S) return, and when will he execute his decision to accompany the forces' commander? Where is the professionalism of the army and the Republican Guards, especially the one we've always heard about? Will the insults and suffering that recruits are said to endure be translated into reality upon me? I wondered if my father succeeded in completing the discharge process from military service after visiting the Ministry of Defence headquarters with the stamped documents I gave to him earlier in the day.

Thoughts collided within me as I drowned in their seas, yet my senses remained vigilant and attentive to my surroundings. Darkness began to creep in gradually. The soldiers gathered around small cargo and pickup vehicles, solemnly listening to the latest news broadcast through the airwaves and radio stations. On this night, U.S. President George W. Bush issued his final warning to the Iraqi President and his sons, instructing them to leave Iraq within 48 hours, or the country would face the shock and horror of a campaign known as Operation Shock and Awe.

Signs of astonishment and despair animated the soldiers. So, the war would commence within 48 hours, and Saddam would not relinquish control of Iraq so easily. Despite my lack of knowledge about the news at that time, the visible signs of bewilderment and anxiety on the soldiers' faces suggested something extremely ominous.

Hours passed gradually, yet I didn't feel any fatigue then; adrenaline still surged in my veins, keeping me alert. However, as time went on, I began to feel pain in my legs and feet cramping. I must have covered several kilometres throughout the day, walking the terrain in front of Adnan's military medical command headquarters building.

Around ten in the evening, with night and silence prevailing in the area, a car approached the headquarters and stopped. Two individuals disembarked. As they got closer, I recognised one of them as Major (S), and the other was a captain. I rendered them the military salute at that moment, and Major (S) smiled, saying, "Hello Choc, hello Doc. How are you now?" I replied in a weary voice, "I'm still waiting for you, Sir. Will you finally send me to the forces' commander? And when will you send me, now or tomorrow morning?" Major (S) gestured for me to follow him and his companion, the captain, into the building, saying, "Come with me to see what I'm going to do with you. Come to the headquarters now. We will discuss your case."

Fear gripped me about what Major (S) intended to do; we had heard many stories about torture and even sexual / assaults / rape of recruits. However, I had no choice but to follow orders. I entered the well-lit room with fluorescent lighting, where Major (S) sat behind his desk, and to his left was the captain, known as Captain Doctor (A), as introduced by Major (S) earlier. I initiated the conversation, saying, "Sir, Major (S), what's the news? What do you plan to do with me?" The light was directed towards my face, making it slightly paler. It was the first time Captain (A) saw me, and both he and Major (S) had dark brown skin. Captain (A) smiled wickedly and meaningfully and addressed Major (S) without paying any attention to me, "Where did you get this cream (milk cream) skinned guy from? He must be mine tonight. Send him to my unit, and I'll take good care of him." Major (S) looked at me and said, "What do you want us to do with you?"

I had lost a lot of strength by then, feeling exhausted due to nervous pressure and walking since midnight. I thought to myself, "Are they hinting at something inappropriate, trying to assault me sexually here?" In a second or two, I contemplated possibilities of escaping. I told myself, "If both of them force me into it, I won't be able to resist for long. How do I get out of this predicament? Should I let them approach and then kick them and escape?" All of this was running through my mind as I answered Major (S), "I want to leave and return to my family.". I have always joked about this with friends in the UK when I told them years later about it. I was always asked what I would have done if they actually tried to sexually assault me. My reply was with a joking tone and a smile: "I was tired anyways, so I might have lowered my trousers and asked them to get on with it quickly so I can get home afterwards before it was too late in the night", to which my friends would burst with a big laughter.

Major (S) asked me, "How much will you pay if I let you go back home now?" I replied slowly, "I only have a few thousand dinars left in my pocket, which may not even be enough for me to take a taxi home at this late hour. But I can give it to you, and I'll pay the taxi when I get home." He smiled and said, "And what about the green bills (referring to U.S. dollar bills)? Don't you have some hundred-dollar bills?" I responded swiftly, "If I had them, I would have paid the full amount to be exempt from military service and get rid of all these problems." He said, "Are you being honest? That's strange. All Christians have relatives outside Iraq and send them money, so how can you tell me you don't have any dollars?" I said, "But I don't have any relatives abroad to do that for me.". Major (S) gave up his attempts and said, "I'm just joking with you; don't believe a word of what I said. Don't believe these things about the army; we don't accept or take bribes in the Republican Guards. I don't want a single penny from you." I told him with a smile, "I know that, Sir, but what does this mean? What will you do to me then?" He replied coldly, "Nothing. You're free. You can go back to your unit or home if you want." I said to him, surprised and questioning within myself if this was one of his tricks: "What? What do you mean? What about the forces' commander? What is his decision?" He said, "Don't worry; I found a doctor for him since 11 in the morning, and you are no longer needed. You can go wherever you want." I told him, "But I don't know the way to the main gate or Unit 40." Then Major (S) turned to Captain (A), saying, "Captain, can you take Dr. Sarmad to Unit 40 on your way back to your unit?" Anxiety crept back into me, "Is this a plan between them for Captain (A) to be alone with me?" Reluctantly, I agreed, as I didn't want to provoke Major (S)'s anger again. In just a few minutes, Captain (A)'s driver sped us away through the night darkness in one of the small cargo vehicles towards Unit 40.

'The Final Escape'

I arrived at the Field Medical Unit 40 around half-past ten in the evening. Major (F.A.) was still awake, along with the enlisted dentist (Z.A.). I informed them of my ordeal, and they granted me a five-day leave to complete the remaining paperwork for my discharge from mandatory military service. Fortunately, the military ambulance was heading to the city of Beiji. Major (F.A.) asked if I wanted a ride to the city so that I could take a taxi to wherever I desired. I sincerely thanked him and I accepted his kind offer, appreciating his cooperation, and understanding of my situation.

As previously explained, Adnan's forces were stationed between the cities of Tikrit and Beiji. The latter housed one of the most prominent oil refineries in Iraq, situated midway on the international road between the capital, Baghdad, and the city of Mosul. Throughout the journey between Unit 40 and the city of Beiji, I contemplated which destination to choose: Baghdad, where my father returned to finalise my discharge procedures at the Ministry of Defence, or Mosul, where my father would go if everything went smoothly at the Ministry of Defence. I decided to return to Mosul; there was no use in heading to Baghdad. Additionally, my mother was alone at our home in Mosul, unaware of our situation. It was crucial to reassure her, especially if communication between Mosul and Baghdad were to be cut off.

The recruits in the ambulance informed me that they were heading to Beiji to shop for necessities for the next day. They offered to drop me off at the main taxi station in the city, from where I could go wherever I pleased. I thanked them profusely and bid them farewell, wishing them good luck in the coming days.

The strategic location of the city of Beiji made it a city that never sleeps, especially the restaurants on both sides of the international road and the main taxi station. Although the station wasn't too crowded by the time I arrived, within minutes, the taxi I had chosen was filled with passengers, and we headed towards Mosul. I informed the driver that I would pay him an additional amount if he took me to my house in the old Noor district on the east side of the Tigris River in Mosul.

From the moment we entered Mosul, it felt like a city of ghosts, shrouded entirely in darkness. No movement on the streets, even those usually bustling, as if the city anticipated an impending storm or doom. I reached home after one-thirty in the morning. My mother wondered what was happening and why I arrived without my father. I briefly explained my challenging day and how my father was completing the procedures in Baghdad. Afterward, we called my father to assure him and my sister's family about my well-being and that I wasn't being held at the headquarters of the forces' commander.

'The Last Day and Night Before the Coalition Military Strike'

On the following day, Tuesday, the 18th of March 2003, in accordance with my father's plan, he headed to the Ministry of Defense to complete the ominous procedures. Afterward, he returned to my sister's house, who, along with her family, had decided to leave Baghdad the previous night following President George W. Bush's warning to Iraq. However, they postponed their departure until my father finished those procedures. The car was loaded with bags and necessities as they set out towards Mosul, including my father, sister, her husband, their few-months-old daughter, and my sister's husband's family. They became guests in our home, leaving my brother-in-law's aunt in charge of household affairs until their return. Despite our efforts to make it seem as if they had not left, my sister's mother-in-law and her sister-in-law could not bear it and returned to Baghdad after a few impatient days.

As soon as my father arrived, we embarked on a journey to find provisions sufficient for the coming days. Learning from the harsh lessons of the 1991 war, we refrained from buying large quantities of meat and poultry, recalling how we had to dispose of large amounts and generously shared more significant quantities with neighbours during power outages caused by the Allies' strikes on power stations. Nevertheless, we had enough supplies to last a few weeks. The goal of that shopping day was to purchase sufficient grains, rice, legumes, and vegetables to feed everyone, and perhaps even the neighbours if they needed anything.

The situation was extremely challenging as food supplies began to deplete from the city's markets. We couldn't acquire everything we needed from a single market, but my father's good relationships with people bore fruit, and some traders in the Ras Al-Jadah area provided us with scarce goods. We also obtained several bottles of liquefied gas for cooking and as fuel for the water heater.

We passed by the Third Recruitment Office in Mosul, only to be shocked to find its doors closed. I initially thought I was late for the scheduled appointments that day, but it turned out that the door was closed, and they didn't receive visitors on that day or the next day, Wednesday, the 19th of March 2003, as I later discovered.

The Wednesday passed quietly, with everyone eagerly monitoring the news through small radio sets, switching between stations like Monte Carlo, London, and Voice of America. The Iraqi TV channels aired national songs, praising Saddam Hussein, along with news and interviews with leaders and ministers. Our refuge was the Syrian television whose clear broadcast easily reached Mosul. Through it, we followed the latest developments in the military situation, the preparations of the coalition forces, Security Council meetings, and news of anti-war protests in the past few weeks.

The hours passed slowly, as if the day refused to end, granting the people a last chance for peace and tranquillity. Perhaps destiny showed mercy, witnessing the impending darkness, violence, and brutality rushing towards them. None of us closed an eye that night. Everyone followed the news through small radio devices, and stations shifted between the different radio stations.

The deadline and warning given to Iraqi President Saddam Hussein and his sons to leave Iraq came to an end. Offers were made to him from the United Arab Emirates and Russia to leave safely, but he strongly refused, preferring not to surrender or bow to his enemies. This eventually led to the entire Iraq bowing before evil and terrorism. Ninety minutes passed after the end of the deadline, and then the air raid sirens blared at precisely half-past five in the morning. Its sound was different this time. It resembled a mournful wail, as if it screamed for help from the impending horror. We waited long but did not hear the sounds of explosions. Did it pass without harm? What happened? Was it a false alarm?

Following the sirens, news reached us, and the U.S. president announced that the first strike had targeted a fortified shelter that was a gathering point for the top leaders of Saddam Hussein's regime, located on a farm in the Dora area. We learned that this farm belonged to Saddam's daughter Raghad. The strike was named the "Opportunity Strike." Thus, George W. Bush declared that the operation to liberate Iraq had begun.

Subsequently, as expected, Saddam Hussein addressed the nation, announcing that he was still alive and speaking about the beginning of the American strike. He said, "Unleash the sword, no fear, no hesitation. Unleash the sword, and let Saturn witness it." He named the next phase "The Confrontation of Fates."

The U.S. administration and the rest of the coalition countries seemed to doubt the credibility of the speech, whether it had indeed come from him or if it was one of his doubles. They expected that the air strike with Tomahawk missiles and B-117 bomb-dropping planes had hit the top authority. However, it later turned out that the supposed shelter did not exist at all.

'Initial War Days'

The official Iraqi radio and television channels broadcasted statements gradually, accompanied by patriotic and stirring songs glorifying President Saddam Hussein. Meanwhile, ground war operations commenced with the British forces landing in Faw, which they easily seized, initiating the Battle of Um Qasr on the 20th of March 2003, following the occupation of the Al-Bakr port. The resistance in Um Qasr seemed formidable. The official Syrian television covered the war events through a daily live broadcast, utilising political and military analysts. We followed the Syrian TV instead of the official Iraqi media, as it presented the latest developments, unlike the Iraqi media's manipulated portrayal for its citizens. The images of resistance in Um Qasr came through the Syrian television in real-time. The British forces attempted to storm the city, but Iraqi resistance compelled some British soldiers to retreat and flee.

The next three days witnessed intense airstrikes on cities such as Baghdad, Tikrit, and Mosul. The General Intelligence building in Mosul was relentlessly bombarded, creating a crater at its former site where onlookers gathered to witness the destruction of this headquarters. Iraqi television showcased war prisoners, including the American Jessica Lynch, and announced significant victories and massive destruction of coalition forces. Simultaneously, foreign radios reported that American forces had penetrated approximately 240 kilometres into Iraq, with battles erupting on the outskirts of Nasiriyah in southern Iraq and attempts to control Basra and Maysan. The rapid news and events left us in a military and political dizziness due to their conflicting nature. How could the British face fierce resistance in Um Qasr while coalition forces advance this far into Iraq, crossing the Euphrates to the opposite bank? And how could the coalition forces declare the surrender of the 51st Brigade in southern Iraq while Iraqi and Syrian media portray it as the force fighting in Um Qasr and near Basra?

Accompanied by my father, I visited the Ras Al-Jadah area, where properties belonging to the ecclesiastical endowment are located. My father supervised these properties by direct assignment from the bishop. We headed there aiming to shop and gather news since some of the relatives of those working there served in the Republican Guards, specifically in Basra. When discussing military actions, one of them informed us that his cousin had called him that day, a colonel in the Republican Guards in the Um Qasr region, reassuring him about the military situation there, claiming everything was under control.

This visit increased our confusion. Whom should we believe? Both sides were undoubtedly lying, yet couldn't there be some partial truth in the military discourse of the warring parties? The state of suspense continued, and Iraq announced that a farmer from the Hindiya region had downed an American Apache helicopter with his simple rifle which was scientifically impossible. Meanwhile, coalition forces declared the start of the Nasiriyah battles on March 23, 2003, which, according to Iraqi media, witnessed massive losses among coalition forces. However, at the same time, coalition forces announced that they were only about 100 kilometres away from Baghdad, after their Apache helicopters raided the forces of the Medina Division of the Republican Guard stationed near Karbala on March 24, 2003, paving the way for the Third U.S. Infantry Division.

Successive official Iraqi press statements denied the American progress, and despite my disagreement with the Iraqi Information Minister, I acknowledged that he performed his job in a way that would have been envied even by Goebbels, the propaganda chief in Nazi Germany. Nevertheless, I also saw him responsible for the loss of many young lives, as he declared the resilience of Iraqi forces and expected the war to end with the defeat of coalition forces or at least with Saddam remaining in power.

Opinions clashed, and the Syrian television reached a point where I vividly remember one of the talk show hosts who hosted a military strategic analyst, asking, "Who do we believe from both sides?" The analyst answered naively, "Of course, the Iraqi side. It is our duty to believe them."

I awaited the incoming news and the image of the leave granted to me two days before the war, looming in front of me. The leave had ended, and I had to join the unit. But isn't this a form of voluntary suicide in such circumstances? Rumours started leaking that some senior Ba'ath Party officials, backed by groups of Saddam's fedayeen, were conducting inspections searching for deserters and those absent from military service. Upon finding one, they staged a mock trial and executed the absent recruit in front of his house. We couldn't be sure about these rumours; perhaps the Ba'athists were spreading them to coerce recruits into joining their fighting units.

Amidst all this, a fellow doctor, (M.T.), from the same military unit visited me. He had found himself in the same situation regarding paying the cash allowance and the procedures for his discharge from military service. He recounted how the commanding officer of the 40th Medical Field Unit, Major Doctor (A.A.), had contacted him, informing him of the necessity to report to the unit and promising him an extended leave. (M.T.) visited me wearing the military uniform, having just returned from the military unit's headquarters to deliver an oral message from Major (A.A.). The message stated that he was pleading with me to visit the unit because, until that day, he had been covering for my absence for two consecutive days. However, he wouldn't be able to do so for the third day in a row. He would have to report my absence to the military leadership, stating that I was absent and failed to join the unit, potentially leading to severe consequences if my name reached the security and Ba'athist authorities in Mosul. It might end up with me as a lifeless body at the entrance of our house there.

I asked Dr. (M.T.) about the situation in the unit and whether there was any guarantee that Major (A.A.) would grant me an extended leave. His positive response mentioned that he had given all those who began the process of the allowance and exemption from military service long leaves. He promised to do the same for me and others in a similar situation. However, the condition was that we visit the unit ourselves; otherwise, he would face punishment for covering up our evasion. When I inquired about the rumours of immediate execution for those evading military service, (M.T.) confirmed hearing the same rumours. Therefore, he urged me to hurry and join them if I wanted to catch up at their current location. Apparently, Adnan forces were preparing to move towards Baghdad within a few days.

This visit occurred on March 25, 2003, and it heightened my certainty about the gravity of the situation and the audacity of the Iraqi president and his leadership. With the veracity of most of the news about the coalition forces nearing Baghdad, the Iraqi leadership decided to withdraw the Republican Guards forces from the north of Baghdad. This was after the deception of a strong attack from the west was debunked, causing the Iraqi president to scatter some units of the Republican Guards near Tikrit and north of Baghdad, placing them on standby to counter the alleged attack. Therefore, the Iraqi leadership decided to redistribute the Republican Guards forces to face the advancing coalition forces deep inside Iraqi territory from the south. But wouldn't the coalition aircraft hunt down Adnan's armoured divisions as they attempted to move towards Baghdad and its outskirts?!

'In the Eye of the Storm'

The visit from my comrade (M.T.) became the focal point of discussion with my family on the afternoon of March 25, 2003. My sister's husband strongly opposed, and my mother was frantic about my suggestion to go. My father hesitated, then insisted on accompanying me. My decision was resolute. I had decided to go to the unit. If death was inevitable, I would face it with honour like a man. I couldn't bear the sight of my parents witnessing my execution. If I am to die in this battle, let me die with honour without bringing shame to my family's name. I didn't want to be captured and killed by murderer released from prison a few months ago to join militias seeking revenge on the community around them. Yet, at the same time, I couldn't dissuade my father from his decision to accompany me.

Before the sunrise on March 26, I was with my father in the main taxi station in Mosul, preparing to travel to Baghdad chasing my unit. We decided to go to Tikrit, and from there, we would rent a private taxi to search for the 40th Medical Field Unit. We reached Tikrit and found the taxi that would take us on our quest. We agreed with the driver to stay with us throughout the search. We reached Tikrit in two and a half hours and found a private taxi explaining to the driver our mission. The driver, a young man of impeccable morals, was exceedingly kind. He understood what was meant for him to do and expressed great cooperation. My father asked for his name, and he replied, "Tawfiq." Which translates to 'Success'. My father then said, "we will then succeed in our mission through God's help," considering our driver's name an omen of good fortune.

Initially, we went to the unit's headquarters, where I had left it last. There was no one there except a few soldiers who informed us that the forces had moved with their equipment and vehicles. The medical units followed them to new locations after receiving the order to move the night before. They had departed at dawn, while these soldiers were the last to remain and would follow them shortly. We inquired about the forces' destination and where we could catch up with them and their final location. The soldiers' answers were shocking and conflicting. One pointed south towards Baghdad, another indicated they would guard Baghdad from within, and the last mentioned they would be positioned on the western side of Baghdad. I commented that the soldiers' answers were surprising, coming from those who would join their forces shortly. They seemed to have no idea where they were going and what the mission of the forces they were part of entailed. Some might argue that these details might not be fully conveyed to recruits, but personally, I found it somewhat strange.

It was a little bit dusty and winds were mild to moderate as we left Mosul, but as soon as we crossed the city of Beiji, the air felt like we were in the midst of a sandstorm. Thick dust filled the air, making breathing difficult. I began to worry about my 71-year-old father with chronic heart and artery diseases, but thankfully, he was not affected by the weather. What was genuinely affected, however, were our military forces' vehicles. Dozens of tanks were overturned on the sides of the road. Most of them did not appear to have been hit by the coalition forces' aerial fire. Some were flipped on one side, while others were completely upside down, and some had their gun barrels stuck in mud and dirt. Occasionally, we saw tank transporters on the right side of the road, with the armoured vehicle or tank they carried tilting slightly, almost tipping over. This scene repeated along the road, and these sightings increased as we approached Baghdad. Katyusha rocket launchers with their carriers and vehicles were scattered on the right side of the road, sometimes under some trees, and occasionally exposed. One of the soldiers lay beneath one of them, and water, and perhaps other fluids, flowed from somewhere beneath the vehicle's body. At that moment, I didn't realise the danger of moving within these short metres of these vehicles, as they were easy targets for the coalition aircraft. I only grasped it after watching some television reports and the extent of the massive airstrikes that hit most of the Iraqi military vehicles. I dared to step out of the taxi and approached these soldiers to inquire about my unit. Everyone I asked pointed out that the forces had headed towards Baghdad and might have reached the south of the capital. We didn't lose hope. The driver, Tawfiq, promised us he would continue with us to the south of Baghdad if necessary.

After a while, we found ourselves behind a military four-wheel-drive vehicle with a specific number, and it had stopped on the side of the road. Tawfiq, without our asking, stopped our car as if he had begun to act like a close family member. He occasionally approached and asked about the 40th Medical Field Unit. This time, he didn't ask, as the four-wheel-drive vehicle seemed to belong to one of the forces. I barely waited before swiftly jumping out of the car before it came to a complete stop. I went to the right side of the vehicle and saluted, introducing myself and my unit and began to ask about its location. As I did this, the rear right seat window slowly lowered, revealing the face of Major (S), with a stern expression and piercing eyes sparking with intensity. It was evident that tension filled the air inside the car. I caught a glimpse of the military rank of the person sitting next to Major (S), a Brigadier General. I thought to myself: It must be the Commander of the forces, Sufian Maher Hasan Al-Tikriti. I saluted again, barely starting to ask about my unit, when the rear right seat window rose, and the car sped away at full speed, leaving additional dust on top of the storm's dust. I stood there for a few moments, then returned to the taxi to share what happened with my father and driver Tawfiq.

By then, we had passed the town of Balad for quite some time, and not much distance remained to reach the village of Tarmiyah and the Taji barracks north of Baghdad. So, we agreed that despite Major (S) not responding to my question, we must have been close to the location of the forces and medical units belonging to its brigade. We decided to continue our journey, focusing more on any military vehicle or car, hoping to find our way.

‘Finally, We Found It’

We approached Tarmiya, and the driver, Tawfiq, was driving at a speed slightly below average to be able to stop when finding any trace of the military unit. I had started to lose hope a bit, as there was no sign so far, except for some armoured vehicles, rocket launchers, and destroyed or damaged tanks, overturned without any signs of being hit by coalition airstrikes. Some had been left by their crews, while others had one or two soldiers standing beside them. We had to slow down a bit as we passed through the highway that cuts through Tarmiya. There were markets on both sides of the road with many passing and parked cars along the markets and numerous shoppers.

It was 10 AM. As we passed near a shop, I spotted a military ambulance parked under a nearby tree. Shortly after, I saw a military four-wheel-drive vehicle attempting to stop on the side of the road. Again, I didn't wait for Tawfiq to completely stop the car, as he had also noticed the military four-wheel-drive vehicle. I quickly got off and rushed to give the military salute to the officer who had just disembarked from the military four-wheel-drive vehicle. He had approached the rear side of it, and I was facing his back. He turned to face me, and there was Major (F.A.), the assistant commander of my unit, and a broad smile appeared on my face as I greeted him more like a brother than a recruit addressing his commander. I informed him of my arrival and found that he was aware of my situation from the colleague (M.T.), who had promised the commander and his assistant to convey their verbal message to me. He was very happy because I didn't let them down, and Major (A.A.) and I didn't allow them to face punishment, which could lead to death, due to their covering for my absence in the previous two days.

Another familiar face emerged from the car, and it was the soldier (Z.A.), the dentist. We shook hands and exchanged the latest information about the military situation. It was evident that they lacked information about what was really happening, and they had no news about the southern front. Instead, they began questioning me, a guy who was about 400 kilometres north, about the conditions in the south, which was closer to them.

While we were exchanging words, Major (F.A.) noted that the paper form granting leave, allowing for an extended leave of ten days or two weeks at once, was in a secure compartment in his car. However, the key was with one of the officer's deputies, who was accompanying Major (A.A) and one of his associates on a mission they would return from shortly.

Despite my joy at meeting Major (F.A.) and dentist (Z.A.), I couldn't help but notice the smell of death spreading in the area. I almost asserted that the angel of death appeared to me, moving without feet, with his black shroud, throwing me a gesture as if to say, "You are to follow if you haven't moved away quickly from this place"

Everything hinted at death, destruction, and randomness, as if it were a miniature image of Iraq suffering the throes of death, as a country dying and exhaling its last breath.

All of this drowned out my hearing for a strange distant buzzing, and then I noticed white threads in the sky above us, moving behind a small metallic body. I asked those around me about the nature of these threads and metallic objects. The answer came from one of them: "Oh, the Barracks of Taji (which is 5-10 minutes south). As I followed the American missiles with my eyes, I noticed coalition forces' aircraft manoeuvring very high in the sky like small objects, then launching missiles from a distance to somewhere southwest of our location. I asked, "And what is this?" The dentist (Z.A.) replied coldly, "Don't worry; these are American planes bombing our 40th armoured Brigade, which is scattered 10-15 minutes by car to the west of our location, and some other forces deployed to the southwest as well." As I tried to absorb what I was watching, an officer with the rank of captain rushed shouting, "Get away from the main road; you'll all be exposed to bombardment. Then he pointed to the sky, saying, "Be careful; there are spotted paratroopers from the coalition forces landing nearby to the northeast of our location. Move away now." We all hurried and ran to where the trees and orchards were on the eastern side of the road. There, I began to glimpse some doctors from my study colleagues and military ambulances. The deputy officer (A.) was wearing a military helmet and holding a Russian-made Kalashnikov machine gun in his hand, and finally, I found one of my friends, Dr. (M.A.), one of the graduates of my class and my colleagues in the military medical school, so we exchanged greetings.

(M.A.), was one of the calm colleagues with whom I spent nearly nine years studying without ever witnessing, even once, any foul language or being part of any problem involving him. Anxiety and fear were evident on his face as he inquired about Mosul's news. I reassured him about the city's well-being before he moved on to inquire about the military situation. Not wanting to exacerbate his clear concern, I said, "Don't worry, our Iraqi radio reports that the coalition forces have not yet crossed beyond Um Qasr in the south. Syrian television is highlighting fierce resistance in the south, and perhaps there's a solution coming soon." (M.A.) came back asking in a concerned and suspecting voice: "What about the coalition countries' radio stations?" Unable to continue pretending that everything was fine more than this, I tried to soften my response, saying, "They claim to have made some progress in southern Iraq, but no one really knows the truth of what's happening anyway." I knew I was lying and hiding the truth a bit, but I did it out of pity for him and his anxiety. I suggested to him to try to leave as soon as possible and return to his family in Mosul, as no one knows where the truth lies. It would be safer for him to attempt to get a leave, as I was trying, and I would be happy to share the taxi with him to go back to Mosul. Despair showed on his face, and he answered me that he wouldn't be able to and wasn't willing to return. He wanted to stay there until the end, as he hadn't paid the cash alternative for military service.

As I reflect now on all that happened on that day, I remember how surreal the situation felt back then. The missiles and aircrafts of the coalition forces were bombing our barracks and armoured forces, while the reactions of those around me were cold, devoid of any feelings, just like those who have accustomed to scenes of destruction. Though I harboured no feelings of love or hate for Saddam's regime at that time, the pain squeezed my heart for a country dying bit by bit, losing its dignity, and its ruins scattering like the pieces of Adnan's forces' vehicles and tanks caught by the coalition aircrafts fire. The honour of the country was stained with the shame of an unjust, unparalleled, and humiliating military defeat that Iraq as a nation wouldn't be able to recover from anytime soon.

The coldness around me and the fire of anger and internal pain were mixed with the colours of the sandstorm that had started the day before and still had some traces lingering between clear periods giving a bleak look to the day. They appeared amidst the scent of repulsive death, adding to that strange place filled with people gathered by fate in those critical moments a crazy, almost Daliesque, atmosphere. Surrealism that leads you to the brink of hysterical laughter and choking with tears of anguish simultaneously. Surrealism that affected and continues to influence my personality, inner self, thought process, and reactions since that time. I became an extremely calm person, and no situation rattles me anymore, even if it is death itself, for how can death rattle me when I've seen it, breathed its air, and smelled its putrid odour? But at the same time, that experience worsened my psychological state due to the nervous pressure I faced that day.

I thought to myself at that moment, is this the end? Will I die here? It seems that death in this place and at that time would be a fitting conclusion for the preceding days and all that I had been through in the past weeks was as if a movie director was organising all these events according to a prewritten script. Indeed, it seemed the most logical end at the time.

'The Final Extortion'

After an excruciating period of waiting, a military four-wheel-drive vehicle arrived, bearing the commanding officer, Major (A.A.), whom I greeted with enthusiasm. I presented him with a bundle of money, cleverly disguised as a gift to avoid arousing suspicion, informing him that it was a simple gift from my mother. Major (A.A.) smiled, gesturing towards the front of the vehicle for me to place the bundle there. As I handed another bundle of money to Major (F.A.), I turned my attention to Major (A.A.) asking about the fortified safe's key which led to a shocking revelation by him – the key was still with the deputy officer associate who had not returned with Major (A.A.), still occupied with some tasks and might be delayed in returning.

I questioned the two officers, "What do we do now? The situation here grows more perilous with every passing moment. Can't we borrow some models from other units? Are there no other models in another location besides that safe?" The response was a firm “No”, but Major (A.A.) suggested giving me two models, meaning two regular leaves, each with the maximum duration of five days, totalling ten days. The idea intrigued me, but I was anxious if the war extended beyond those ten days, so I asked, "What if the war persists beyond this?". Major (A.A.) looked around, as if scrutinising for eavesdroppers, then spoke in a hushed voice, "It probably won't last longer, but even if it does, all you have to do is return here, and we'll grant you another leave. I give you my word. Moreover, this location appears to be our final position, making it easy for you to find us next time if you need to come during the war."

I had no choice but to agree, realising that prolonged waiting might expose me and my awaited father in the taxi to airstrikes targeting our unit or any military convoy passing through the area. Additionally, hearing of the possible U.S. Army paratroopers landing, as the Captain did point out to a short while ago, hinted at the imminent closure of the roads by the coalition forces.

The papers were stamped and signed swiftly. I greeted everyone, exchanged quick farewells with some friends and colleagues before leaving that area. As I turned, eager to reach the main road where my father and the taxi awaited, someone called my name. I turned, anxiously, to see Captain Doctor (A.) sitting in the front seat of an ambulance, with the door left open, alongside the infantry Captain I mentioned earlier. I hurried toward them, saluting and hoping this would be my last salute for the day. Captain (A.) inquired, smiling with his usual sly smile, about my news and activities, asking if I had been granted the leave. I responded briefly, attempting to conclude the conversation swiftly. His companion started, "Did you have breakfast this morning, Dr. Sarmad?". I answered, "Yes, Sir." He continued, "Would it please you to know that your fellow recruits haven't had any food or breakfast until now, and it's already past eleven-thirty in the morning?". Realising his intentions, I replied, "Of course not." Infantry Captain (A.) then suggested, still smiling, "Why don't you go and buy them breakfast from the nearby shops, or better yet, give us some money, and we'll buy them something to eat ourselves. What do you think?". Tired of this form of blackmail, I responded, "Alright, I'll go and buy some Qaimar (a traditional Iraqi version of clotted cream made from Iraqi buffalo whole milk), honey, and fresh bread from the nearby store, and I'll be back immediately." The infantry captain feigned surprise, saying, "What? Qaimar and bread? Oh, deary me, these guys want kebabs, kebabs. Do you know what kebabs are?" Despite his suggestive remarks and gestures, I tried to ignore them, stating, "No problem. I only have seven thousand dinars left in my pocket, equivalent to less than five US dollars at that time. You can come and get approximately two kebabs portions for them. Unfortunately, I don't have any more money." I revealed the lining of my military trousers' pocket to convince him that I had no more money. The Infantry Captain watched as I did this, still pretending to smile, "Seven thousand dinars? What do we do with that? It won't be enough for even two of these starving men, and it's already past eleven-thirty in the morning! But okay, leave it here; give it to us, and we'll handle it." Ignoring his implications, I handed them the money, and started running back to the taxi, caring only about escaping that insane place, thinking to myself, "People are dying, and the country is burning around this damn place, and this filthy man thinking of extorting seven thousand dinars from me (which was less than five US dollars at that time). Do we have the right to ask why this happened and why this kind of guys hate almost everyone in Iraq, forcing Iraqis to hate them and the regime at the same time?"

'A Triumphant Return'

I didn't stop running until the I arrived at the taxi, and I said urgently to the driver, Tawfiq, "Get us out of here as fast as you can." I turned to my father, pointing to my pocket where I kept the leave forms, saying, "We succeeded in what we came for; I got the leave."

As soon as the car set off, I had already taken off the military uniform I wore over my civilian clothes. I didn't want a checkpoint of either our Iraqi forces suspecting me of being a fleeing military recruit or an American checkpoint, which might have been deployed to block the international road between Baghdad and Mosul could arrest or kill everyone in the car because of me.

On the journey back to Tikrit, I was more aware of what was happening around us on the road, no longer preoccupied with finding the military unit. Dozens, if not hundreds, of vehicles were fleeing from the impending hell approaching Baghdad. All loaded with bags and used mattresses, resembling a mass exodus of the city's residents. I also noticed the staggering number of Adnan Force vehicles that had been either disabled, stopped, or deliberately halted, as inferred from the position of the vehicles and the expressions of the soldiers around them.

We thanked Tawfiq profusely after leaving him at the taxi station in Tikrit, where he dropped us off. My father rewarded him generously for his high professionalism and dedication. It only took a few minutes before we were on our way back to Mosul in another taxi, where we arrived home around three in the afternoon amidst ecstatic joy from everyone, especially my mother, who spent the day praying for our safe return. We hadn't finished lunch when one of my uncles called to check on my safe return with my father, inviting us to visit them at their home.

Upon visiting them in the afternoon, my uncle's family gathered around my father and me as soon as we arrived. My uncle hugged me tightly, shedding a tear, thanking God for our safe arrival. Both families listened attentively to our story of what we faced and witnessed on our journey, especially since the news stations claimed that the Iraqi president's regime had successfully transported military units from the Republican Guards from the north of the capital to Baghdad and its outskirts, taking advantage of the sandstorm over the past two days. The shock was greater when we narrated the state of the tanks and other vehicles we found on the international road to Baghdad.

Their astonishment peaked when I told them about the condition of my military unit, the confusion and indifference prevailing. The armoured brigade's vehicles and our barracks were being bombarded continuously. I described the panic evident among most of the recruits, the officers' lack of concern for the situation, and some of them continuing to exploit the vulnerable recruits whenever there was an opportunity for it.

During the years that followed, telling my friends and colleagues about those challenging days always took on a distinctive character. As I would narrate these events and details, my colleagues' reactions ranged from being astonished by the horror of the shocks that Iraq endured and that I personally experienced, to others being incredulous, and some expressing amazement at the humour with which I recounted certain events, even if they were from the most difficult situations.

On one occasion, while six of my colleagues and I were having lunch during a break from work at a hospital in Britain, the conversation turned to the 2003 war. When some of them learned that I had memories of it through my military service, questions began flying from here and there, attempting to learn more about the events of those days from someone like me who had lived through and witnessed them firsthand. During the tale of my journey to the Tarmiyah region, where I found the Medical Field Unit 40, one of them asked if I had fought or managed to kill any soldiers from the coalition forces during that time.

Due to the loud noises around us and being distracted by consecutive inquiries from here and there, I didn't fully understand the question at first and thought that my colleague was asking about the number of Iraqi soldiers killed in that war, especially since the previous question was related to losses in equipment and vehicles Iraq had encountered in that war when I recounted seeing many of our tanks embedded in the mud on the sides of the international road leading to Baghdad and the coalition airstrikes targeting our armoured brigade. Therefore, I answered the subsequent question with an approximate number, saying, maybe fifty thousand.

A heavy silence and dumbfounded expressions covered the faces of all my colleagues, some of them British and from other European nationalities, initially bewildered by the simplicity with which I – an Iraqi guy – spoke about killing fifty thousand people. Everyone momentarily believed they were facing a ruthless war criminal and a dangerous and cunning murderer who had managed for a long time to deceive them by appearing as a peaceful and friendly person.

One of my hesitant colleagues broke the silence after several moments, asking if I was responsible for a missile launch unit to be able to kill all those soldiers in that short war. Because it was impossible to kill such a large number in those few days with a personal weapon or even an automatic weapon, the reason for the silence and astonishment on the faces of my colleagues became clear. I then clarified the misunderstanding, and the place exploded with laughter and loud chuckles at the misinterpretation that had occurred.

'The Coalition Forces' Offensive Continues'

The ground offensive by the coalition forces paused for a while as the sandstorm that covered the south of Iraq and its deserts between March 25 and 27, 2003, had subsided. It was also a moment to catch their breath and extend the supply lines after advancing deep into Iraqi territory, akin to a hot knife cutting through butter. Simultaneously, the coalition forces continued to engage Iraqi forces, aiming to wear them down before delivering a final blow. Fierce battles raged near the city of Nasiriyah to destroy what remained of what was known as Ali's Ambush set by the Iraqi forces. Additionally, in Najaf and Karbala, elements of the Third American Division emerged, seemingly out of the desert west of Karbala. They orchestrated two attacks, one as a diversionary tactic away from the true destination, heading south of Baghdad through the city of Hilla. The main thrust of the attack aimed to approach the Karbala Gap (of the Iraqi Republican Guards forces) situated between the city itself and Lake Tharthar. This strategic move left the Iraqi Republican Guards forces stationed there, particularly the forces from the Al-Medina Al-Munawarah division, in a state of confusion on how to distribute their units. This confusion delayed their response to the main American strike, which aimed to approach and seize control of Baghdad Airport for its symbolic and strategic importance, followed by capturing the presidential palace complex on the Tigris River afterwards.

While the First Marine Division advanced from Kut and faced the Baghdad Division of the Republican Guards to encircle Baghdad from the east, some paratroopers from the 173rd Airborne Brigade were deployed in northern Iraq to establish the northern front. This happened after the Turkish Parliament rejected the use of Turkish territory for the ground assault, preventing the establishment of this front before this airborne operation.

These days witnessed painful bombardments of Baghdad, Basra, Mosul, and some other cities, targeting command and control centres of the Iraqi army, the Republican Guards, Saddam's Fedayeen forces, and the Ba'ath Party. This was a continuation of the bombing that began on the second day of the war. In one of these airstrikes, while I was fast asleep in my room on the first floor of our house around three in the early morning, a massive explosion resounded, shaking the foundations of the house. It threw me from my bed to the ground, and truth be told, to this day, I don't know if it happened due to the intensity of the shock or the force of the explosion. By morning, we saw the aftermath of the destruction that befell the headquarters of the Iraqi Doctors Syndicate in Mosul, which was about a kilometre away from our house. This headquarters had been occupied by Saddam's Fedayeen forces, turning it into their headquarters just days before the war.

The headquarters had been hit by highly destructive missiles, transforming the large two-story building with a beautiful design into rubble consisting of partially destroyed concrete columns and remnants of walls. As if this strike was not enough for the coalition forces, the same site was hit again by a similar strike a couple of nights later. Fortunately, I had left my room after realising the danger of sleeping in it in such circumstances. My bed was under the window of the room, and it wouldn't have shielded me from the flying shards of glass that were scattered and could have embedded into my body had I stayed. We used brown adhesive tapes to secure all the glass panels in the windows of our house from the aerial bombardment of the coalition forces. So, my experience with the first airstrike prompted me to sleep in one of the ground floor rooms away from any windows. However, this did not prevent my panic from sleeping again after the second strike, which turned the remaining structure of building struck earlier into debris that was level with the ground due to second missile strikes on that night.

Rumours circulated in the city of Mosul indicating the use of mobile phones, of the type used by some, belonging to the Thuraya company. These rumours suggested that some spies threw these phones or electronic chips inside some of the Iraqi security / intelligence headquarters for the coalition forces to hit them shortly afterward with precise and focused missile strikes.

‘The Siege of Baghdad from the South’

In the midst of the battles in the city of Najaf, the Youth Television, owned and operated by Udai Saddam Hussein, the eldest son of the former Iraqi president, broadcasted live coverage of the unfolding events. The presenter, Abdulhakim Za’lan, commented on the live events from the rooftop of one of the houses there. The transmitted images in the background showed an Apache helicopter manoeuvring over locations in the city, while the Iraqi announcer declared, "These helicopters are being hunted down one by one, and this one shown in the background is the last remaining from this squadron, and it will be swiftly brought down." I was in shock on how the Iraqi media tried to obscure the clear reality with such foolish reporting. Having Apache helicopters roaming Najaf's sky means at least that the coalition forces are much closer than what the these media outlets are reporting and the fall of the regime is definitely imminent.

As the Iraqi forces faced these relentless strikes and losses, the Iraqi Minister of Information, Mohammed Saeed Al-Sahhaf, announced the severing of the American forces – he dubbed (American snake's) – spine and the disruption of their supply lines. He, along with the Iraqi media, spoke of hundreds of casualties among the coalition forces' fighters, the downing of dozens of aircrafts and helicopters, and the disabling of a similar number of tanks and military vehicles.

In summary, reality became entangled with fantasy. Despite my assurance in the accuracy of the news about the coalition forces nearing Baghdad, deep inside, I found myself hoping for the resilience of the Iraqi forces. Yet, that would mean exposing myself to danger if I attempted to rejoin my military unit in the prolonged war. I couldn't discern if it was pride in my country, an excess of nationalism and idealism, or simply a reluctance for change and perhaps fear of what the future might hold due to the impending change.

Tuesday, April 1, 2003, witnessed two pivotal events strategically on the military stage. The first was the liberation by coalition forces of American soldiers who had been captured on March 23, 2003. Among them was the nineteen-year-old American, Jessica Lynch, whose image was broadcasted on Iraqi television alongside her comrades. The signs of shock and panic were evident on their faces, anticipating an unknown fate – a move that had a significantly negative echo in Western media, even among those who opposed the war. It reflected a considerable misjudgement by the Iraqi leadership of the situation and a profound misunderstanding of Western society, further solidifying the image of the Iraqi regime as one steeped in oppression and tyranny.

The second event marked the commencement of ground confrontations near the city of Karbala between American forces and the Republican Guards. This included forces from the Al-Medina Al-Munawarah Division stationed there, which had been completely exhausted by consecutive airstrikes in the days preceding, making them easily bypassed afterward.

The deceptive attack on the city of Hilla, despite the American forces expecting it to be an easy stroll, encountered resistance that lasted longer than anticipated. Nevertheless, this courageous resistance was brutally crushed due to the concentrated firepower of the American forces. They overcame it afterwards easily, thanks to the density of the American forces' fire from the south of Baghdad. Thus, Baghdad found itself under complete siege and cut off from southern Iraq. The Third American Army crossed the Karbala Gap and the Euphrates River to the east bank, approaching from the south of Baghdad, while the Marines advanced from the east after surpassing Baghdad's Republican Guards forces deployed near Kut. Soon, the southern part of Baghdad was encircled from all sides by all these advancing forces.

'Heavy Days Tinged with Fear'

The following days unfolded like a burdensome dream, marked by continuous power outages, relying entirely on electricity generators for residential areas. Simultaneously, there was a struggle to secure the household's needs, exacerbated by the increased population of the city with those fleeing Baghdad for a safer option. Despite our apprehensions of a potential airstrike directed at the primary school located just 70 meters from our house – the one I attended in my childhood – that had been occupied by Saddam's fedayeen militias. They had stacked weaponry and equipment endlessly in the converted classrooms turned into storerooms for those piles.

As the thirty-first day of March 2003 approached, the first five-day leave granted to me by the Major (A.A.) came to an end, leaving me with another of the same duration. Conflicting news at that time led me to count the hours and minutes remaining on my deadline. I attempted to track news about Adnan's brigade and its affiliated medical field unit 40. Yet, nothing could ease the anxiety, whether from the Iraqi media or the bits of information from the coalition forces' countries media that reached us through the radio.

Occasionally, I ventured out with family members to assess the city's situation. The visible aftermath of airstrikes marked some areas, yet overall, the city seemed to proceed quietly toward its fate without any immediate signs of trouble.

Our sole source of concern, as a religious minority, was the control exerted by religious extremists, known for their significant presence in Mosul. They would definitely dictate the course of civilian life, regardless of the war's outcome, and whether Saddam Hussein and his regime were overthrown or managed to stay in power. These extremists had spread throughout the state's structures, multiplying in numbers since the mid-'90s. They caused suffering for religious minorities in the city.

Mosul had been known for its Sufism and religious moderation until the late '70s. However, with the rise of Salafist and Brotherhood movements, particularly during the '80s, religious extremism began to trouble even moderate Muslims. Despite this, the minorities found solace in the fact that the state, as an institution, did not officially practice any form of persecution. Secular rule, under the iron grip of the Ba'ath Party, prevailed, suppressing any individual attempts by these religious extremists.

As the central state's power waned and its nationalists and Arab ethnic support popularity dwindled after the occupation of Kuwait, the Iraqi regime was forced to compromise its secular principles. It turned a blind eye to the actions of extremists, ensuring the loyalty of those who openly spread within state institutions in the '90s.

This tolerance allowed them to approach seizing control of Mosul unofficially, awaiting an opportunity for the regime's grip to loosen.

This situation caused constant headaches for moderates and minorities who had grown accustomed to peaceful coexistence with peers, experiencing few problems in the past. Thus, a confrontation between conflicting interests and visions was inevitable. Saddam Hussein's regime acted as a safety valve, preventing this confrontation from surfacing. However, the fears of moderates and minorities stemmed from the fact that even with him in power, the rise of extremists had escalated in the years leading up to those crucial moments. If the coalition forces left Saddam in power again, as they did in 1991 after Iraq's invasion of Kuwait, two seemingly contradictory yet intricately connected outcomes would occur.

The first was the regime's increasing reliance on extremists, and the second was the exploitation of these extremists seizing the opportunity to overthrow the regime step by step, possibly all at once, racing against time.

All of this occupied a significant part of my thoughts during those days when I buried my emotions and thoughts in computer games, in a strange and ironic contradiction. I escaped from the harsh realities of war into strategic war games. I was astonished when playing one, where the beginning spoke of a coalition forces' assault on the city of Um Qasr, and these forces wandered into southern Iraq to complete their occupation. Following that, they encountered forces or militias seemingly affiliated with Saddam's fedayeen. These militias set up ambushes and numerous obstacles, mimicking what actually happened almost two years after the production of this electronic game, whose name, if memory serves me right, was "Black Gold."

'The End of the Iraqi Regime is Nigh'

Between the 1st and the 6th of April 2003, several cities in southern Iraq fell one after another slipping from the Iraqi regime's hand like beads falling off a broken chain or necklace, such as Basra, Najaf, and Kut. However, the most notable event was the Battle of the Airport, surrounded by a great deal of confusion. Reports of its capture by the 3rd American Army circulated, while other forces were allegedly involved, obscuring many facts about the situation. On the 3rd of April 2003, American forces were within about 10-20 kilometres west of Baghdad, infiltrating the outskirts of Saddam (Baghdad) International Airport to occupy parts of it. However, a tactical operation by the Iraqi Special Guards forces, commanded by Saddam's younger son Qusay Saddam Hussein, in collaboration with Saddam's fedayeen militias, utilised a deception that fooled the American forces into believing that the Iraqis were using chemical weapons. This led the American soldiers to don protective masks, impairing their vison to some degree, and the Iraqi soldiers and fedayeen militants aggressively attacked them. It turned into a fierce battle with white weapons, and while the American forces seemingly suffered significant losses, Iraq lost some of its elite units and well-trained troops. Despite briefly reclaiming the airport by the Iraqi forces, the devastating losses incurred prompted the order to withdraw the Special forces and what remained of the Special Guards back to inside Baghdad, leaving the situation in the hands of less capable forces, unable to withstand the second surprise attack by American forces on the 4th of April. Thus, the American forces took control of the airport and its facilities on the 5th and 6th of April. Many of these fedayeen as well as the rest of the Iraqi forces responsible for defending the airport even those who managed to escape the last American troops offensive were captured after the withdrawal of the Special Guards.

The bloody scene was, of course, not broadcast to us in the rest of the Iraqi cities. However, echoes of the events, initially denied and later downplayed by Iraqi Information Minister Mohammed Saeed Al-Sahhaf, reached our ears through radio stations. The official Syrian television presented conflicting perspectives, but it neither could nor perhaps wanted to confirm or deny either narrative.

Although we had tuned in to several radio stations in the city of Mosul, one image could speak volumes. Thus, you can conclude that the nearly complete isolation of the city from the world was astonishing. No visual news hinted at what was happening in Baghdad, and we no longer received the live broadcast of Iraqi terrestrial television. All that reached us was a rebroadcast through a local station in Mosul, but even this broadcast consisted mainly of patriotic songs glorifying Saddam, without interruption.

The American forces took control of the Al-Radwaniyah Presidential Palace, and the U.S. Marines succeeded in crossing the Tigris River from the east, surrounding Baghdad from the east, south, and west. They established control, awaiting the major battle – the Battle of Baghdad itself. Here, the people of Baghdad held their breaths, anticipating urban warfare in the alleys and streets of the city, with uncertainty looming.

In those critical moments, everyone was asking about the whereabouts of the Iraqi President Saddam Hussein and whether he was still alive. Did he succeed in escaping with his family? Was he still in Baghdad? Where were his close associates? Numerous rumours surfaced, claiming to have seen him personally fighting at the airport, launching anti-tank missiles at American forces. Others insisted that he met his demise there, engaged in battle. Meanwhile, some asserted he had fled to Syria or Russia. The rumours continued until he appeared in the Mansour area of Baghdad, addressing a gathering of citizens chanting for his life.

Amidst these rapidly unfolding events, my thoughts turned to my colleagues and friends, (W.M.) and (A.Y.). I called Dr. (W.M.), who had been assigned to the Republican Guards forces in one of the medical field units attached to the Hammurabi Division near the city of Kirkuk. Relief filled my chest when I heard his voice over the phone when I called enquiring about his well-being. He had been absent from his military unit since the outbreak of the war and was untroubled by the consequences. Now, he was eagerly awaiting the fall of the Iraqi regime.

On the other hand, our colleague Dr. (A.Y.) had not returned to Mosul yet. I learned from his mother that he had not been discharged from the Military Medical School, and he had been transferred to the Rashid Military Hospital in Baghdad. He was stranded there, with his father, the renowned physics teacher (Y.A.), having travelled there two days before my call to bring him back. However, they were both stranded there, and communication had been cut off with them, with no news from that area.

Our colleague (M.A.) had stayed with Field Medical Unit 40, which had been moved and directed to the south of Baghdad. However, they were intercepted by an American armoured patrol, and their members dispersed in military ambulances. One of these ambulances carried our colleague (M.A.), and it attempted to evade the patrol by taking a shortcut. However, what the driver didn't anticipate was spotting American tanks on the opposite side. He swiftly made a U-turn, driving against the traffic. Fortunately, the highway was empty at that moment, but unfortunately, the American tanks had noticed them and started chasing. Our colleague (M.A.) was beside the driver, and his astonishment grew as the American tanks approached the military ambulance while its speed exceeded 120 kilometres per hour, unusual for such military vehicles in Iraq. Finally, the driver managed to escape his pursuers by taking one of the exits on the highway, leading them to a residential area that helped them conceal themselves in its side streets while the American patrols passed by, moving away.

A colleague from the dental department later recounted his adventures in one of the southern Iraqi cities, where the divisions of the Republican Guards he had been assigned to were scattered. Due to that many soldiers from those forces escaped the firing by the American forces, the commander had to resort to guerrilla warfare against the American forces, utilising the dense palm groves in the area. Recruits climbed to the tops of palm trees to strike American armoured vehicles roaming the area. They succeeded in disabling two, but the air support arrived in the form of Apache helicopters, which began to comb the area. Realising that the situation was becoming dangerous, the commander had to allow the remaining few recruits to disperse and withdraw. They returned safely to their families after the majority of their forces were effectively eliminated.

'The End of the Leave Period'

The surreal situation and the desperate nightmare we were living in continued at that time with racing events, but the situation in Mosul remained stable despite the successive losses of the Iraqi regime in some southern cities and the imminent loss of Baghdad. The Fifth Corps stationed near Mosul, at the Khazir River axis, was still almost intact, albeit having faced sporadic shelling, which forced it to withdraw about ten kilometres from its original positions. However, unlike other Iraqi military units that had disintegrated in the preceding days due to the intensity of American fire and the destructive power of the coalition forces' weaponry, the Fifth Corps held its ground. The morale of the remaining Iraqi soldiers had suffered significantly from the continuous and relentless attacks that did not give them a chance to catch their breath.

The fifth of April 2003 arrived, and with its sunset, the second leave I had obtained from my unit's commander, Major (A.A), came to an end. As this day concluded, the perplexing question emerged: What is my fate now? Rumours of arresting those who evade military service and executing them had intensified, especially after a speech by Iraqi President Saddam Hussein urging fighters to join any combat unit near them if they were unable to rejoin their original units.

The news of the battle and the American advance was no longer a secret, making us realise that it was only a matter of days before the regime fell in Baghdad. However, this did not mean its final collapse, as it still controlled the northern and northwest provinces of Iraq, with their vast areas and human resources fiercely loyal to it, such as Anbar, Salah El-Din, and Nineveh (with Mosul as its centre). These provinces and their cities were a significant source of strength for the regime, not to be underestimated.

Therefore, the regime's grip on Mosul had not loosened yet, and the members of its militias, whether Baathists or fedayeen, still controlled the fate of the city and its people. Their presence in our neighbourhood, at least through the nearby school they had occupied as an alternative site, was palpable. A recurring question cut through our thoughts at that time: Would the city witness street warfare in the coming days if the American forces, supported by the Kurdish Peshmerga forces, advanced? The sense of hostility towards anything different in terms of nationality or belief had reached levels we had not anticipated during our days in Mosul, indicating the potential for a massacre if the potential confrontation turned into urban gang warfare.

I tried to avoid the possibility of arrest, so on the sixth of April 2003, I headed to the Republican Educational Hospital (also known as Al-Zahrawi) where I had spent the recent period of my work before joining the military service. I had established a network of distinguished relationships with the surgical staff there, especially the postgraduate students, whom I asked that day to admit me to the hospital as a patient with an acute surgical condition. They hesitated, fearing legal consequences since I was a military person, not a civilian. This meant that a civilian hospital was not authorised to treat me, only to provide necessary first aid and refer the military personnel to the nearest military hospital for further treatment.

There was a single loophole: the emergency appendectomy due to its urgency, requiring immediate surgical intervention. My colleagues assured me of their willingness to perform the surgery as a last resort in case I did not receive an official leave from any military doctor. They also provided me with admission papers to the hospital as evidence in case I was stopped by any Baathist or fedayeen units / checkpoints.

On the next day, along with my uncle the doctor and professor at the College of Medicine, we headed to Mosul Military Hospital but none of the doctors there could help. We, therefore, decided to head to Erbil Military hospital that was transferred to an alternative location near Saddam Hospital (known afterwards as Al-Salam) in Mosul. We headed there immediately, but we couldn't approach the hospital as a nearby building was hit by an airstrike, and everyone was evacuated from the hospital. Chaos prevailed, and military doctors, in their military uniforms, watched from a distance as black smoke rose from the bombed structure.

Among these doctors was a military doctor with the rank of colonel who, in addition to his work at Mosul Military Hospital, also taught at the College of Medicine - Mosul University. My uncle and I approached him, inquiring about what was happening and if he can help with my situation. He told us that he could not speak freely as we were surrounded by a large number of recruits and other military doctors. Once the place cleared a bit, he whispered to us, looking right and left, directing his words to me, saying, "Wait, don't rush. It won't take longer, just wait for two days, and the situation may turn out to be fine for you."

'The Toppling of the Idol'

News arrived on the eighth of April 2003 of American tanks roaming the streets of Baghdad. It was even said that they had seized important buildings like the Ministry of Information, but Iraqi Information Minister Al-Sahhaf appeared in front of the Palestine Meridian Hotel and denied those rumours. Little did we know in Mosul, where we watched his press conference on the official Syrian television screen, that the American tanks were close to the location of that press conference. They had roamed in Baghdad, crossing the Tigris on the Republic Bridge, showcasing their might to impact the morale of the remaining followers of the Iraqi regime. Although some American vehicles incurred some losses while passing through the Dora area, the ultimate result was that Baghdad had fallen under the mercy of the coalition forces, attempting to capture or corner the remaining members of the Iraqi leadership.

The ninth of April 2003 began peacefully, with a beautiful daytime and the warm April sun streaming through scattered clouds. The family of my middle sister's husband (B.A.) uncle visited our home; they had fled Baghdad in the early days of the war, seeking refuge in Mosul. One of the cousins of my sister's husband whispered with him about how they followed the fall of Saddam Hussein's statue in Firdos Square that morning. My sister's husband was astonished, listening to her account. Her mother intervened, seemingly still afraid of Saddam Hussein's grip, saying, "We don't know anything, we haven't seen anything. We were just told, but nothing is confirmed," despite her daughter confessing to following the events through some satellite channels at their relatives' home.

Wanting to confirm, we switched the television to the official Syrian channel that covered the events in real-time. The coverage continued, with an anchor leading a discussion with a guest, discussing Baghdad's resilience and the expected losses among American forces. Suddenly, the coverage was cut to broadcast the latest updates from Baghdad. The collapse of Saddam Hussein's statue in Firdos Square was shown, assisted by American vehicles, smashed by Iraqi onlookers afterward. The famous Syrian presenter Azza Al-Shar'a announced, with a clear sense of confusion, the evident news of the regime's fall as Baghdad fell into the hands of the coalition forces. She shed a tear as she delivered the news.

The Syrian television then abruptly cut its coverage to broadcast a mournful and sad song by the Iraqi singer Yas Kheder, saying, "Azaz Edna Azaz, which translates to dear to our hearts" A tear welled up at the corner of my eye upon hearing the song, and I turned spontaneously to the rest of the family. Amidst my astonishment, I observed them wiping their tears as well.

So, the idol fell. The regime that had achieved much for the country but also cost much had fallen Perhaps it cost more than it achieved. It had created a hostile environment, laying the groundwork for the dark period that would follow in Iraq's history.

A sense of sadness enveloped everything around me, even the relief I expected to feel if the regime fell was not translated into reality. Despite my reservations about Saddam Hussein's regime, I had wished for a different, less tragic end, hoping it would reform itself and lead the country without resorting to the rivers of blood that were shed. Despite my criticisms of the Iraqi army, its thunderous fall in three weeks did not only affect its dignity but touched the dignity of every patriotic Iraqi. Despite the dominance of the Tikriti family over all aspects of life in Iraq, especially the military and security headquarters, these institutions, despite being subjected to this family's control and serving its interests, still represented Iraq as a state in the end. Iraq, the land of Hammurabi, Nebuchadnezzar, Ashurbanipal, and Samir Amees, a civilization of 7,000 years, had fallen. I felt that the armies of Sumer, Akkad, Assyria, and Babylon, which used to terrify the forces of entire nations with few fighters, were the ones defeated or couldn't inspire their descendants with the needed motivation, strength, and support. My way of thinking might be that of an idealist or utopian, but that's how I love Iraq as a homeland and a country, giving no importance to any other considerations, no matter what they are.

'The Madness Begins'

The day unfolded in astonishment and anticipation, wondering what would happen next, but the calm in Mosul remained unchanged. Despite the fall of Baghdad and its regime, it didn't necessarily mean that the remaining cities to the north and northwest would surrender without a fight. The regime had allies and supporters who, we believed, would resist until their last breath, or so we thought.

The city of Kirkuk, with its vast gas and oil reserves, also fell. On the tenth of April 2003, the Fifth Corps signed a surrender agreement, unbeknownst to the vast majority of Mosul's residents, surrendering the next day. Until the tenth of April, the symbols of the state, Saddam's regime, and its government were still present in Mosul. Ba'athists in their olive uniforms roamed the city, and the police remained in their positions. The fedayeen still occupied their headquarters or at least those who held the school near us.

The morning of April eleventh, 2003, started like any other morning until it was disrupted by the sounds of commotion gradually growing louder. I rushed to the rooftop of our house to see what was happening outside, and dozens were rushing towards the school where the fedayeen were. I jumped to the ground floor and headed straight to the kitchen door overlooking the street leading to the school. My father and the husband of my middle sister (B.A.) were trying to figure out the situation. We decided to go out to the street to understand what was going on. Many residents from specific houses, apart from a few known for their good reputation, were racing into the school only to come out minutes later carrying various firearms and items.

Two neighbours' sons passed in front of us carrying a large bag filled with ammunition. One of the neighbours, a well-known figure who had appeared on TV multiple times urging people towards piety and righteousness, congratulated his son returning from school with his loot – a Kalashnikov AK-47 automatic rifle, handed to him to enter their house together. Another ran with a heavy machine gun, while his brother followed with ammunition in live bullet casings. Within minutes, the street was filled with hundreds of people we had never seen before, apparently launching an attack from the neighbouring districts on the precious stash of weapons inside this school.

My sister's husband (B.A.), eager for reconnaissance, decided to go to the school to see what was happening up close. I still remember my father's shout from inside the house, telling me not to let him in if he came back with anything looted from the school, and that he would not allow anyone, even if he was his daughter's husband, to tarnish his reputation at this age.

My lifelong friend and neighbour (M.S.) crossed the street from his house opposite ours (one of the families that did not stain their hands with looting weapons from the school). We exchanged a mix of sarcastic and ironically funny conversation about what was happening before our eyes. As we talked, a teenager we had not seen before, not older than fourteen, passed by carrying a mortar. We asked him what he planned to do with such a weapon, not a pistol or an automatic rifle he could use for self-defence or to protect his family. He replied that he and his group knew what they were doing and would use it at the right time. Confusion and mockery were evident in our faces as we watched him and some of his seemingly friends move away from us, playing and tossing hand grenades among themselves. I turned to my friend with a question, and the confusion and mockery were evident in my voice as I said, "They know what they'll do with it at the right time?!" My friend (M.S.) responded with a smile and the same mocking tone, saying, "Perhaps they'll use them in a war between neighbourhoods after a slight argument among their children about a football game, so they decide to shell each other's houses to settle matters."

We learned later that the fedayeen had left their position in the school after taking what they could of the best weapons early in the morning. The locals then came to what remained of the weapons after the continuous looting operations. After a while, a small pickup truck arrived carrying several individuals who seemed Kurdish telling by their outfits. They began firing into the air to disperse the crowds gathering around the school. Mrs. (R), the school principal, rushed from her nearby house to where we stood, then ran to the school, bewildered and shouting, "They stole my school, they looted my school!"

My friend (M.S.) and I watched the chaos that affected almost everyone around us as if a contagious disease had spread overnight among the residents of our area and its surroundings. As if the fall of the regime unleashed a group of demons or monsters from their cages, giving the green light to the complete collapse of the moral system of society as a whole. As if the fall of the regime militarily announced the general collapse of the social system, turning the overall situation into a literal translation of the phrase "the fall of the system," which had become a fall in every sense of the word.

That day, I felt the true meaning of feeling insecure, and for the first time, I felt real fear. All the challenges in my life until that moment had never made me feel such a mixture of fear and unease, blended with anger. Even in the darkest circumstances, even when Major (S) tried to force me to accompany the leader of Adnan's forces, even when I smelled the scent of death, and the U.S. forces pounded the Iraqi forces and barracks around us, I never felt something akin to that disgusting feeling. But those insane moments frightened me and made me realise how many monsters lurked around us without us feeling it until someone unlocks their jaws or breaks the chains that bound them, unleashing their ferocity. They would bare their fangs and devour everything around them, both the good and the bad, turning everything beautiful into darkness, casting a pitch-black shadow over their lives and the lives of those around them.

‘The Madness and Chaos Extend into the City’

The bizarre scene persisted for some time, and I returned indoors after my sister's husband (B.A.) came back from school, fortunately, without any stolen weapon or object. His morals seemed above such temptations, and he successfully passed my sister's tests, eventually becoming her husband. He, too, was astonished, but his curiosity led him to explore what was happening across Mosul. He decided to roam in his car, but my father insisted on accompanying him.

They returned after a few hours, recounting gruesome scenes and events they witnessed with their own eyes. Mosul University was being looted, the latest computers were plundered from the colleges, furniture was loaded onto the backs of cars and transported away from all government buildings. Banks were being looted, and bags of money were being taken out of the banks in hundreds. They described how they watched someone enter a bank, come out with a bag of money, and throw it away upon discovering it contained only 25 Iraqi dinars bills. This process repeated until he found a bag with 10,000 Iraqi dinars bills, which he carried away, leaving the other bags by the roadside.

Those who stole the money bags later discovered that some of them contained defective notes that should have been destroyed due to printing errors, such as identical serial numbers. Some of them decided to sell these bundles in exchange for old and smaller denomination notes. The one million dinars, consisting of 10,000 dinar bills, would be sold for half a million dinars or a similar amount in smaller denominations in currency exchange shops or on the streets.

Even electrical appliances, like air conditioners securely attached to buildings, were forcibly removed and disconnected from their protection systems, which were often cut with electric saws. Some thieves did not venture far from the crime scene but stood on the opposite sidewalk displaying their loot for sale. One might attempt to sell a stolen fan or computer as if it were a television. Other stories from my acquaintances confirmed that the staff offices in colleges and government departments, with sensitive and confidential information about the employees, were scattered everywhere after being scattered by the looters. Some patriots tried to collect these documents and papers and store them in their homes until life returned to some semblance of normalcy. Thus, madness and a state of decay spread throughout the city.

My father and (B.A.)'s narratives painted a grim picture of the city, making me feel more insecure and terrified. This was not an ordinary fear or a personal terror of anything that might directly impact my life or the lives of those around me. Instead, it was a horror of what had befallen the society surrounding us. At that moment, I realised the true impact of over 12 years of economic sanctions, shifting the balance of morals for this society as much as it crushed the economic status of the poor.

More than 20 years of consecutive wars and the bloodshed that filled the hearts of the country's children and youths with brutality, thirst, and an accustomedness to the sight of blood. My realisation of the true extent of the general moral decline of society frightened me, and the danger of this decline became apparent, ominously foreshadowing what was expected to happen in the coming years.

The local television station in Mosul began broadcasting again after being taken over by a person from those opposing Saddam's regime called Mashan Al-Jubouri. He aired daily recordings and speeches to explain what was happening in the city, criticising Saddam Hussein's regime policies, and discussing the forthcoming change and his vision for the future. He also showcased recorded programs from satellite news channels like Al Jazeera and Al Arabiya, and the famous program at the time, "From Iraq," hosted by the Lebanese presenter Eli Nakouzi, who exposed the inhumane and deviant practices of Saddam Hussein's regime. Other programs aimed to influence Saddam's popularity among his supporters were also aired.

'Guardians, Thieves or Both?'

Amidst the brutality of robberies and irrational practices committed during that insane period, the actions of the minority of good-hearted individuals among the Iraqi people, specifically in Mosul, stood out. They alleviated the horror of our shock at society's descent into chaos. Some from this virtuous group took it upon themselves to protect certain state facilities and departments as much as possible from the treachery of marauding gangs and looters. These groups took advantage of the complete absence of state authority and security apparatus, such as the police, who abandoned their posts, fearing retaliatory actions from criminal gangs. In the face of this, some small groups resisted the plundering of some hospitals.

The ironic and laughable aftermath of the looting of state departments and schools was the formation of popular committees, announced to protect neighbourhoods. This was a response to the fear that theft and looting would spread to citizens' homes. Ironically, these committees were formed by those who had been looting and plundering just hours before their formation. It was both comical and tragic at the same time.

Due to the municipal departments, including essential services, ceasing operations during the war, waste and filth piled up in designated barrels in front of homes. Their stench clogged noses, forewarning of a humanitarian disaster and the spread of diseases through flies that were sure to multiply in such fertile breeding grounds. People decided to dispose of the waste themselves and began transporting it in their vehicles to waste disposal sites.

On the twelfth of April 2003, with my sister's husband (B.A.), we decided to dispose of the accumulated waste in a garbage barrel at our house. We distributed it into some boxes, which we placed in the back of (B.A.)'s car, intending to head to the nearest waste disposal site. Committees of young people from the area were formed to search all passing cars for stolen items. Members of these committees were the same individuals from the neighbourhood who had been looting the school and weapons shortly before. As (B.A.) drove us in the car, youths at a checkpoint about 10 meters away noticed that the rear box of the car was slightly open. Despite knowing that we hadn't stolen anything and had just left home, they stopped the car under the threat of stolen weapons from the previous day, holding some makeshift weapons and knives. We stopped immediately, facing their question about what was in the box and whether it contained stolen goods. I got out of the car, answering that it was "garbage, and we're trying to get rid of it." They didn't believe us and requested permission to fully open the box to verify. I nodded affirmatively, unable to hide a smirk of mockery on my face as they were shocked by the sight and smell of the waste they had tried to cover up while signalling for us to hurry and move on. (B.A.) drove the car again amid our laughter, saying in unison: "Guardians and thieves at the same time."

Looting continued in Mosul, unfortunately, mirroring the situation in other cities across Iraq. Rumours circulated that American forces were opening the doors of state institutions and encouraging people to loot. However, it was confirmed that the looting and plundering were carried out by Iraqis, a statement I make with deep shame and regret. Every night, we followed the news through the bulletins of Al Jazeera and Al Arabiya which stated that at least one official Iraqi building, such as a museum or ministry, was looted to its last possessions. Oh, the shame, as our dirty laundry was aired in front of the whole world.

'Return to Medical Duty'

A campaign began on local television in Mosul on the twelfth of April 2003, urging those absent from work in state institutions, including doctors and medical staff in particular, to return and join their hospitals and workplaces. I had been contemplating returning to work since the previous day, and the call came as a decisive moment for me. I would return to work, and I would visit the Provincial Health Department, offering my services voluntarily if needed. At that moment, I felt that my place was not in front of the television at home. The city needed everyone capable of working to rebuild it, and the nation needed all experiences to bring a glimmer of hope and compensate for the dark and grim image left by the preceding days, a bitterness I still feel all these years later.

The next day, with the cheerful morning promises of spring, I headed to the Nineveh Health Department. The personnel in the Individuals Affairs Department informed me of their approval for my temporary assignment to the last hospital where I worked before joining military service, emphasising that this assignment would be without any salary for now until my official and formal reinstatement. I agreed immediately, surprising the personnel in the department, and headed to the hospital, which was only a five-minute drive from that Department. There, I was assigned to work in the Third General Surgery Unit, where the regular resident was absent for several days without any communication or apology. I covered for his absence for the entire day.

On the following morning, I met the doctor in charge of junior doctors (Dr. S.A.), and we discussed many issues that had occurred in the past few weeks. He was one of the dear colleagues I had worked with for five months in the Second General Surgery Unit in the same hospital less than a year before. He was kind and fully aware of the situation I might be in due to the events of the previous weeks. He asked me if I would like to work in the emergency department, as they were in need of someone with my experience, given the numerous absences the hospital had in that department. They were forced to rely on inexperienced doctors, some with barely a few months after graduation, to handle the massive influx of patients and some challenging cases resulting from injuries among civilians facing armed gangs and a shortage of some medical supplies.

I didn't think long about the offer, as I found it suitable for me. Working in the emergency department meant working in shifts for a few continuous hours, followed by a day off. I didn't want to work in one of the wards that required me to stay continuously in the hospital for more than a day, possibly for several days, without checking on my family at home. What motivated me even more was that the offered shifts were from the afternoon until midnight. Other doctors on shift in the emergency department continued to work until the morning, meaning I could return home on the same day. Typically, those shifts were between 4:00 PM and 10:00 PM.

I agreed immediately to Dr. (S.A.)'s offer without realising at that moment that the emergency department's shift system had changed slightly, extending the shift until midnight. However, despite that, it did not affect my decision, and I never regretted it.

'Medical Service Adventures - Part 1'

Dr. (S.A.) handed me the schedule for the shifts, signalling my return the next day before 4:00 PM to take over the emergency department. As I entered the department's building, I noticed a group of American soldiers sitting on the right side of the emergency department's waiting area, across from the doctors' on-call room. Later, I learned that their military unit had been requested to station some of them to protect the hospital after several attempts to steal and attack it, along with attacking the medical staff, by gangs of looters and thugs.

The medical staff in the emergency unit informed me that on the night of the tenth and the eleventh of April 2003, which witnessed the looting of Baath Party headquarters and state institutions, things had completely spiralled out of control. As night fell on these two days, groups of thugs and looters attempted to approach the hospital, aiming to loot it while carrying weapons. This forced the police station personnel near the hospital to flee, leaving the hospital at the mercy of these looters. Yet, some hospital own security personnel and nursing staff resisted, defending the hospital with personal weapons left by the police or owned personally by tyhem. Some even continued to perform their medical duties, treating patients while carrying weapons openly on their backs.

I heard other stories about how some gangsters entered the hospital carrying hand grenades, heading straight to the doctors' on-call room without paying the fees. They would then order the on-call doctor to prescribe powerful sedatives in large doses under the threat of their weapons. The situation escalated to the point where they forced surgeons to perform operations on their relatives without waiting for their turn in the operating room schedule, disregarding the critical condition of other patients. They did all of this while holding their weapons in front of or pointing them at the surgeon's head.

One of the looters with his gang, after being confronted by a defending group while attempting to steal from some residential areas and cars belonging to the locals, got his brother injured by gunfire. He carried him, along with his weapon, to our hospital immediately, without permission, to the emergency surgical cases monitoring room. Dr. (S.A.) was the surgeon in charge of the emergency unit for that day, along with some other doctors, between a senior resident and a regular resident. Dr. (S.A.) volunteered to examine the wounded, only to find that he had alreadt passed away. He tried to convey the news to his accompanying brother, who was still carrying his automatic rifle. The latter suffered a nervous breakdown and began firing continuously from the muzzle of his weapon, aimed in front of him, not at any target. Eventually, he ran out of ammunition while all the doctors, patients, and visitors lay on the ground. The robber continued shouting, threatening, and intimidating until the hospital guards finally managed to apprehend him while he was attempting to change the ammunition store of his weapon. The result was decorating the room's wall with bullet marks and damaging some medical devices. After that, some doctors and other staff refused to return to work there.

Working in the hospitals at that time was madness, but this didn't prevent me from going there to fulfil my duty almost daily or as required by the shift schedule. I wanted the goodwill in society to overcome the sudden emergence of evil in the past few days. I wanted to see exemplary models from colleagues who, like me, decided to prioritise the country's interests over our own, even if it meant risking our lives. We bought fuel for our cars at exorbitant prices from the black market to reach our workplace. Personally, I never thought for a moment about any financial benefit from this service. I can say, on behalf of all those I worked with at that time, that the same applies to all colleagues.

The working hours were hectic and very busy with all kinds of medical cases. The congestion was severe, prompting some doctors to send patients to the emergency internal medicine follow-up hall without examination or even writing any notes on the patients' records, causing distress and anger to some senior residents. The crowding escalated in the hall beyond the capacity of the doctors responsible for this unit in the department. When working in the emergency reception, dozens of patients and their companions would gather in the on-call doctors' room without adhering to a queue or any system. I confess that the situation lacked any professionalism, but we provided our services based on the available resources.

The American soldiers rarely interfered with our work most of the time. They spent most of their time sipping soft drinks and cold juices, then aligning metal containers to form pyramids on top of each other.

The only time they did something was when the number of patients increased, and they rushed to enter the emergency department, pushing and shoving to get in. At that moment, they would organise the patients into lines and queues only when we, the doctors, asked them to do so. They would then rise from their positions immediately to arrange the lines, sometimes enjoying forcing people to adhere to the queues and stand in an orderly manner.

One of the funniest incidents that occurred while the American soldiers responsible for protecting the emergency department were present happened one night when we heard gunshots near the hospital. The American soldiers came out to the entrance of the emergency department, lying on the ground amid the sounds of gunfire, some chanting and ululating. Meanwhile, we all stood nearby in a normal manner, suppressing our laughter, as it was clear that the source of the gunfire was a wedding procession, a detestable Iraqi tradition of firing live rounds into the air to celebrate weddings. The American soldiers remained lying down for about a quarter of an hour while we tried to tell them the truth of the situation, and they didn't believe us. Some of them even said that we were a crazy people until their leadership's command centre reassured them after sending a military force that intercepted the wedding procession. The certain news reached them about the reality of the situation.

In the beginning, American soldiers would seek the assistance of the medical staff when apprehending a looter near the hospital to help with translation during the interrogation. I was asked once to help them with translation and investigation. The apprehended person had his face covered and his hands tied. The matter did not last more than a few minutes; as an American army vehicle arrived, everyone boarded it, and they disappeared within seconds.

'Medical Service Adventures - Part 2'

In one of my early shifts in the emergency department – the emergency surgery ward, a senior resident in orthopaedics, Dr. (A.A.), whom I had worked with before, asked for my assistance regarding a patient in the emergency surgery ward. Dr. (A.A.) informed me that he had a patient with a deep wound on one of his legs, and after confirming the absence of bone injuries or bleeding from major blood vessels, he wanted me to suture the wound. He justified this request by highlighting the lack of experience among the rotating residents in the surgery ward and the busyness of the senior residents with some emergency surgeries.

I requested him to at least provide me with an assistant or someone from the medical or nursing staff to help me in the upcoming task. However, he explained that the majority of them were absent for one reason or another on that day. Despite feeling uneasy, I eventually agreed to save the situation, especially after he promised to arrange for another doctor to take care of my patients while I completed suturing the wound.

Dr. (A.A.) accompanied me to the room where the patient was, introducing me briefly to him and his family. Signs of agitation were evident in the patient, who was speaking excessively. As I approached him, the smell of alcohol emanated from every part of his body. He threatened Dr. (A.A.) as he attempted to leave, looking at me with disdain and mockery. He asked if I would be the one stitching up his wound, and I responded succinctly, avoiding provoking his anger. I went to fetch the suturing kit, returning a few minutes later to find him still ranting, foaming at the mouth, and rambling nervously.

It was clear that the patient had been involved in a knife fight, as superficial scratches covered his arms. However, this deep wound on his leg was the most severe and posed a threat to his life due to the potential for rapid infection if left open without suturing.

I informed his family that I needed their help to restrain him while I sutured the wound since he was still under the influence of intoxicants and in a state of drunkenness, making it impossible to predict his reaction during the procedure, especially since he had attempted to strike me as I approached while laughing and giggling.

Fortunately, he had two strong relatives who agreed to stabilize his upper and lower extremities, allowing him only minimal and simple movements. However, his relatives could not prevent him from showering me with a constant stream of insults, met simultaneously with apologies from his family and relatives.

I proceeded to clean the wound thoroughly, removing dead skin, dirt, and coagulated blood. Luckily, and fortunately for the patient, I found no evidence of injury to major blood vessels in that area, meaning that the patient's condition would only require a routine suturing. With each stitch, I anticipated a sudden attack or him grabbing the instruments to stab me. However, his robust relatives managed to restrain his upper and lower extremities, allowing him only limited and simple movements.

I finished suturing the wound after a few minutes and headed to the special operating room in the emergency department to hand over the patient's papers to the senior resident in the emergency surgery ward. To my surprise, I found all the residents from the emergency surgery ward, both seniors and rotating ones, along with Dr. (A.A.), waiting for me. All the resident doctors had refused to suture the patient, fearing him, leaving me in this prank that stirred some anger in me, but I thanked God for the safe passage of the day.

'Medical Service Adventures - Part 3'

In the early days following the fall of Saddam's regime, as American soldiers observed the events unfolding in the emergency department, I commenced my duties in the chaos. A patient arrived, suffering from a severe heart attack, accompanied by his wife. Without waiting for the nurses or assigned personnel, I had the patient lie on one of the mobile beds. I personally wheeled him to the critical care unit and sprinted back to the pharmacy, gathering the necessary treatments and medications for the patient. I returned without leaving him until he began receiving treatment, surrendering him to the care of the duty physician.

Two days after this incident, the American sergeant in charge of the group guarding the department questioned soldiers and staff about the ownership of a car parked near the emergency gate. To his surprise, I was identified as the owner. He exclaimed, "No way, unbelievable, I can't believe it." When I inquired about the reason for his disbelief, he informed me that some had reported that the car parked near the emergency gate was rigged with explosives. Upon learning it was mine, he couldn't fathom that the doctor who rushed to save a single patient two days ago would attempt to harm a large group of people. Therefore, he decided not to inspect the car, convinced I would never commit such horrible act. Despite my relief at his trust, over time, I felt I had erred by not insisting he thoroughly inspect the vehicle. Perhaps someone had planted a bomb to incite chaos or attack the American soldiers protecting the emergency department at that time. Consequently, I asked the American sergeant in charge of the night shift to inspect it himself. Reluctantly, he agreed, and I accompanied him to the car. He asked me to open the doors and step back as he thoroughly examined it, confirming its complete absence of explosive devices.

One of my shifts in the emergency department coincided with the birthday of the former Iraqi president, Saddam Hussein, on April 28, 2003. As the sun set on that day, we began hearing commotion in the nearby neighbourhoods and gunfire. Subsequently, groups of wounded arrived, revealing that they had been shot by supporters of the former president during riots. The supporters of Saddam Hussein engaged in acts of disorder to assert their presence. One of the scenes etched into my memory was speaking to a wounded man who had sustained a gunshot to his head, resulting in part of his brain protruding through the bullet hole. I attempted to reassure and support him while being transferred to the neurosurgery unit at Ibn Sina General Hospital. Among the injured was also a young, talented surgeon whose car was targeted with a gunshot that shattered the front windshield, causing complete loss of one of his eyes.

The events of April 28 unfolded while the doctors in the emergency department were on strike, refusing to treat non-critical cases like colds and such, demanding attention to only critical cases instead. This was initiated by some general surgery specialists in the hospital, who asked the American forces responsible for protecting the hospital to stop this practice. This led to assaults on the medical staff, and the emergency department was marked by rampant chaos during the shifts. The rotating residents eventually agreed to this strike.

The hospital administration sent one of the senior physicians to negotiate with the rotating residents. We all gathered in the lobby of our residence, and he began talking about his work history and life experiences, downplaying the significance of the problem we were facing. He claimed that we had not experienced any difficulties in our lives compared to what he and those of his age had gone through. After he finished his speech, he inquired about our demands and whether we had a response to his words. My colleagues granted me the permission to speak on their behalf since I was perhaps the oldest present. I addressed the specialist physician and said, "Firstly, I'd like to dispel the notion that our generation has not faced any hardships. Allow me to give you an overview of my own life, which represents the life of our entire generation." I continued to recount the hardships our generation endured, from the eight-year war with Iran to the invasion of Kuwait, the subsequent economic sanctions, and the devastating Gulf War. I emphasised that there was no basis for comparison between the series of events in the lives of individuals from our generation and those in his, which enjoyed years of prosperity and travel, while we were deprived of the most basic necessities for an extended period.

My colleagues attempted to conceal their smiles as they watched the negotiator's facial colour shifting between yellow, green, and red. I countered his arguments with undeniable facts about the recent incidents, how our colleagues were humiliated, and some were physically assaulted while performing their duties. Finally, after hearing testimonies from the assaulted colleagues, an agreement was reached. The hospital administration would formally request the American forces stationed at the Mosul Hotel to send forces to protect the hospital and its staff twenty-four hours a day.

'Fate of my Close Friend (A.Y.)'

The news about Comrade (A.Y.) had vanished completely for a while. All I knew was that his father had to travel to Baghdad to bring him back to Mosul just days before the fall of Baghdad. Yet, they never returned due to the circumstances surrounding the fall of Baghdad and the difficulty of travel between Iraqi cities thereafter.

My friend (A.Y.) had been transferred to the Rashid Military Hospital a few days before the war for his military service. I tried to contact his mother daily to check on him. Finally, some joyful news arrived, indicating his return once he and his father could secure enough fuel for the car.

On the promised day of his return, I went to visit him in the afternoon. I parked the car and knocked on the door of their house, only to find he had gone to a nearby store to buy some necessities. I waited for some time, and as soon as I spotted him returning, I rushed to embrace him warmly.

We spoke about his recent days in Baghdad during the war and what happened before, during, and after. Not being chosen to join the Republican Guards meant he stayed in the Military Medical School until he was discharged after paying the required cash allowance. He had kept going there until he was transferred to the Rashid Military Hospital, east of Baghdad and near the Military Medical School. (A.Y.) had been trying relentlessly to complete the discharge paperwork, facing the same obstacles I had experienced, especially given the time constraints before the outbreak of the war and the subsequent challenges in mobility. He told me about what he heard regarding the Military Medical School, how it was occupied by the U.S. Marine Corps, and how "The Prince of Wrath" (a Brigadier General in the Iraqi Army) was one of the last to resist there even after most recruits and officers had escaped. Eventually, he was killed, according to most reports from that area.

(A.Y.) also spoke about the entry of American forces and their armoured vehicles into Baghdad just days before the fall of the regime, passing through the Dora area. The locals welcomed them joyfully, but suddenly, some insurgents appeared to disable several vehicles, indifferent to the civilians.

We discussed his plans and what he intended to do in the coming days, and in the end, I managed to convince him to return to work at the Republican (Al-Zahrawi) Hospital, which he did.

I attempted to contact Major (A.A.), the commander of the 40th Field Medical Unit, to thank him for his cooperation with me during the war, covering for my absence and subsequently assisting with my leave during the war. His wife answered the phone, and she was very cautious while speaking to me, perhaps fearing targeting due to her husband being one of the members and officers of the Republican Guard by some. In the end, I learned that he had returned safely from the war without any harm befalling him.

After the shifts in the emergency department, it was customary for the ambulance crew to escort the doctors back home, while those with private cars drove themselves home. The ambulance crew accompanied by my friend (A.Y.) during my drive halfway to ensure I wasn't subjected to harassment or a gang trying to rob me. One night, moments after reaching the halfway point and the ambulance crew leaving my car, taking the road leading to the house of Dr (A.Y.), my car's engine suddenly stalled. It was terrifying after the recent incidents of robbery. I hurriedly got out after the car stopped, attempting to restart the engine while opening the hood. I tried repeatedly to reconnect the battery wires as the indications pointed to an electrical problem with the car. Fortunately, the engine roared back to life after I had almost lost all hope. I sped off at my maximum speed to reach home without any further issues.

'The American Protection Unit'

During our time in the emergency department at the Republican Hospital (Al-Zahrawi), we began to get acquainted with the American soldiers tasked with providing security for the hospital and its staff. I still remember soldiers (A.L.) and (K.S.), as well as Sergeant/Corporal (J.H.), along with military doctor (J.S.). What set this group apart was that they were all university graduates with excellent credentials. Sergeant (J.H.), for example, held a degree in basic sciences (qualifying him for further studies in various medical and scientific fields), and he aspired to specialise in marine biology after completing veterinary medicine studies (considered one of the most prestigious specialties) upon his return to the United States. Despite their academic prowess and ethical demeanour, what truly astonished me was their complete ignorance of the conditions in Iraq and the region, coupled with their extreme naivety.

Sergeant (J.H.) worked diligently to keep his group always ready for any emergency. He would call them from the emergency building's location, wherever they were in the hospital, via radio, informing them of an emergency and calculating the time they would spend reaching the site. He would then instruct them to improve their response time.

The last two hours of the evening shift, between ten and midnight, were always characterised by a drop in the number of patient referrals to no more than a handful per hour. To pass the time, we invited the soldiers to sit with us in the doctors' room, exchanging conversations on various topics such as arts, movies, sports, daily life in our respective countries, politics, and recent events in each of our lives in the past few weeks.

During one of the nights, we delved into their experiences during the war, as members of the renowned 101st Airborne Division. I threw an unexpected question about the personal motivation of each of them to come and participate in the war against Iraq. Two of them stumbled, but the third, Private (K.S.), volunteered an answer: "I did this to protect the United States and prevent Saddam Hussein from sending his army to America to fight and harm its citizens." My next question was, "Since you participated in military operations, did you see or feel that the Iraqi army had any capabilities to reach America, let alone cause any harm to its people and military forces?" The three soldiers were momentarily shocked, and Private (K.S.) fell silent, bewildered, as if discovering something previously unknown. He finally said, "Actually, I haven't observed any capabilities of that sort, but that's what we were told by our superiors before coming to Iraq." I smiled, saying, "Someone must have been lying. I wonder who that might be."

The naivety of Private (K.S.)'s response, followed by signs of naivety apparent in all the soldiers I had met, made me pity them. I perceived them as individuals thrown into the fire, unaware of the slightest information about what would be a blatant violation of the basics of military science, requiring soldiers to be familiar with the situation in which they fight and on which they operate.

In other conversations with Sergeant (J.H.), who appeared more outspoken and intelligent, though not significantly more informed than the others, he demonstrated no knowledge of the social structure of Mosul, its neighbourhoods, population composition, and the environment surrounding both his stationed group in the hospital and the one at the nearby Mosul Hotel, which the U.S. forces had turned into their headquarters. He seemed utterly uninterested in performing the duties of an occupying force responsible for the country they had just invaded, attempting to restore some security to its cities, including Mosul. The deteriorating security situation, with a rise in thefts and looting targeting state institutions, became more evident. There were no indications of any intention on the part of these forces to apprehend those involved in these crimes. There was no effort to identify the perpetrators and the neighbourhoods from which they emerged, turning these incidents into a way of life for some rather than attempting to address the destructive results and aftermath the country faced afterward.

Strangely, Sergeant (J.H.), when discussing these conditions with him during the night shifts, did not display any knowledge (as the sergeant in the presumed American forces responsible for managing the affairs of the city and Iraq in general) of the reasons behind the failure to prevent these crimes. We did not understand why there was no effort to recognise the identities of the culprits and the neighbourhoods from which they came. This information was readily available to the ordinary citizens of Mosul and Iraq. Despite Sergeant (J.H.)'s apparent interest in learning about the suspicious neighbourhoods and Mosul's demographic nature, asking about all this to the doctors, his lack of awareness indicated a profound intelligence gap unbefitting of a professional force claiming leadership in the world and also claiming responsibility for governing the country as an occupying state.

His responses sparked doubt and raised questions about their authenticity and whether he truly knew anything about these matters. However, his reactions and facial expressions during our conversations, and him noting down in a small notebook about some of the things we considered common knowledge to him and the U.S. forces, personally shocked me. It revealed a severe deficiency in the American planning for the post-war period.

Our relationship strengthened with some of the American soldiers, and some of them became comfortable in our presence. They would visit the residents' doctors' lounge every night without us inviting them, to talk and spend time together. One night, we invited the protection unit to join us for a feast we prepared in the resident doctors' lounge in the emergency department of the hospital. Each doctor brought a dish famous in Mosul, such as dolma and mumbar (rice and minced meat stuffed in carefully cleaned sheep intestines), with the latter receiving the most comments from the American soldiers, accusing us of eating shit during that meal. Still, the soldiers, in general, recorded their appreciation for the food. I, on the other hand, prepared a dessert that gained approval from both the doctors and the American soldiers, especially Sergeant (J.H.), who claimed it was very similar to a dish he used to have in his hometown in the United States.

'The War Ends, but Other Wars Await'

The war had concluded, unveiling grotesque faces left behind by the preceding years. It opened the door to new wars that awaited Iraqis and awaited me in particular. Later on, memories of this war became child's play, and as a nation, we mourned its days compared to what followed. Religious extremism extended its powerful grip, and the language of force prevailed, with uncertainty and chaos becoming dominant features in the years that followed, making life in this part of the planet more challenging than ever before.

As humans, we faced wars that were not only daily but around the clock. Iraq rapidly treaded towards a future tossed and battered by fierce waves, threatening to erase it from the map of existence and perhaps even beyond time. Many years followed that war, and Iraq still groans under its weight, languishing beneath its burden to this day. Civil wars embellished with fake names, growing animosity among compatriots, and a lack of trust rendered the healing of past wounds nearly impossible, at least in the near future. At one point the country lost a third of Iraq and more than one Iraqi province falling into the hands of a terrorist organisation that nearly consumed what remained of Iraq.

I approached death on multiple occasions, just steps and centimetres away from it at times. Landmines, explosive devices, bullets flying in the air, and the thunderous explosions shaking the places I inhabited. Amidst all this, I lost my father, taken by death after a heart attack caused by the explosion of a car bomb near our home. All of this occurred within the span of two years between 2003 and 2005.

Stay tuned, my dear readers, for the next instalment of memories from the post-2003 period, encompassing all these events, along with the subdued tales brewing beneath the surface of the incidents and horrors of the subsequent years. Until then, I extend my regards to you all.

Printed in Great Britain
by Amazon